PUB WALKS ALONG
The Cornwall Coast Path

TWENTY CIRCULAR COASTAL WALKS

C000059771

Eleanor Smith

COUNTRYSIDE BOOKS
NEWBURY, BERKSHIRE

COUNTRYSIDE BOOKS
3 Catherine Road
Newbury, Berkshire

ISBN 1 85306 459 9

Designed by Graham Whiteman
Maps by Jill Lyman
Photographs by the author

Produced through MRM Associates Ltd., Reading
Printed by J. W. Arrowsmith Ltd., Bristol

Contents

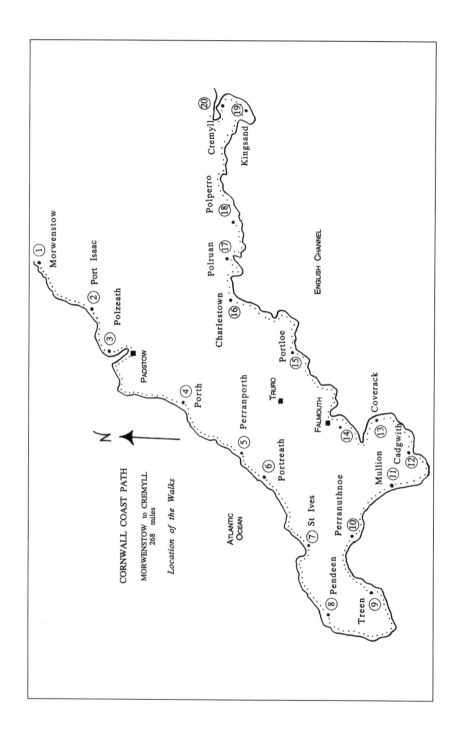

CORNWALL COAST PATH

MORWENSTOW to CREMYLL
268 miles

Location of the Walks

N

ATLANTIC
OCEAN

ENGLISH CHANNEL

① Morwenstow
② Port Isaac
③ Polzeath
PADSTOW
④ Porth
⑤ Perranporth
⑥ Portreath
⑦ St Ives
⑧ Pendeen
⑨ Treen
⑩ Perranuthnoe
⑪ Mullion
⑫ Cadgwith
⑬ Coverack
⑭ FALMOUTH
⑮ Portloe
⑯ Charlestown
⑰ Polruan
⑱ Polperro
⑲ Kingsand
⑳ Cremyll

TRURO

Walk

PUBLISHER'S NOTE

We hope that you obtain considerable enjoyment from this book; great care has been taken in its preparation. However, changes of landlord and actual closures are sadly not uncommon. Likewise, although at the time of publication all routes followed public rights of way or permitted paths, diversion orders can be made and permissions withdrawn.

We cannot of course be held responsible for such diversion orders and any inaccuracies in the text which result from these or any other changes to the routes nor any damage which might result from walkers trespassing on private property. We are anxious though that all details covering the walks and the pubs are kept up to date and would therefore welcome information from readers which would be relevant to future editions.

INTRODUCTION

The South West Coast Path covers a distance of some 515 miles between Minehead in Somerset and Poole Harbour in Dorset. The splendid Cornwall Coast Path is the central portion of the route.

This book is one of a series entitled *Pub Walks Along...* which uses established middle and long distance paths as a basis for shorter circular walks, all easily tackled by the casual walker. Not many people can allow enough time to walk the whole Cornwall Coast Path, which enters Cornwall by a footbridge across a stream at Marsland Mouth between Hartland Point and Bude and leaves it some 268 miles later at the ferry which operates across a deep channel between Cremyll on the Cornish side and Plymouth in Devon. This book provides the opportunity to sample the pleasures of the Path in undemanding, stroll-sized portions, circuits of 3 to 5½ miles, taking no more than a couple of hours each or half a day if you build in plenty of time for stopping and looking. They are ideal family walks and are full of interest.

The Cornwall Coast Path is by no means a new one, parts of it have been in existence from the time when smuggling first began on a nationwide scale and customs officers on horseback maintained surveillance of the coast. Some of the routes which cover the loneliest cliff paths date from this period and other sections came into use as short cuts from one cove to another. During the mining heyday it was used by miners walking from mine to mine. Later the paths became important to the coastguard service who used them to watch for bad weather. They were little used for pleasure until after the First World War. Many of them pass through areas of outstanding natural beauty or of scientific interest, and more than 122 miles are owned by or covenanted to the National Trust. The Path reveals a wide spectrum of both seashore and bird and plant-life particularly appropriate to dunes, clifftops and moorland. You can see fortified promontories where ancient man fled to escape his enemies, and stone circles and standing stones commanding an imposing position on the clifftops. The industrial archaeology of Cornwall is much in evidence along some stretches of the coastline where derelict mine buildings fall into an ivy-clad decay.

As I write there is no official logo for the Path. The Countryside Commission has an acorn as its national logo and this is used on Coast Path signs throughout this route. National Trust signs are represented by an oak leaf. You will see both of these logos as you walk and both will be referred to in the text. For clarity and convenience I have referred to both north and south coast paths as just the 'Coast Path', the demarcation line of which is at present at Penzance.

The River Tamar separates the counties of Devon and Cornwall and this peninsula exhibits a wide variety of terrain. Cliffs in the north rise to heights of over 400ft in total contrast to the south with its sheltered inlets and coves. The wild and rugged Atlantic seaboard compares with the busy shipping lanes of the English Channel. Land's End with its imposing granite formations offers another contrast, as does the Lizard peninsula with its Mediterranean-type plants and lush growth. The Coast Path, generally, follows the clifftop, or in some cases, the beach itself. Care should be taken during high winds or on stormy days and windproof clothing may be called for except during high summer. Certainly strong shoes or boots are a must. If walking on the beach make sure you know the tide pattern and don't risk being cut off.

At the end of each chapter is a section devoted to the long distance walker, with outline directions for the Coast Path route between the pub walks. It includes the position of the ferry points for crossing the various river inlets along the coastline. Where an inland detour has to be made it has been noted in the text. Anyone doing the Coast Path walk will need more detailed maps than those provided here but the book will be useful as a means of locating both overnight accommodation and a meal and a drink en route. And maybe these general descriptions will inspire those who are following the circular walks to fill in the gaps themselves one day!

The pub walks can be undertaken with some confidence using the text and sketch map, which is designed to guide you to the starting point and give a simple yet accurate idea of the route to be taken. However, for those who like the benefit of detailed maps, the relevant Ordnance Survey sheet is very much recommended, especially for identifying the main features of views. There are several from which to choose, but I have given the Landranger (1:50 000) number in each case.

Some of the pubs used are typical country 'locals' while others, in busy tourist areas, are geared to the holidaymaker and serve fast food. Many have a children's play area. All have been sampled by the writer and her husband and are included because they not only have a good circular walk nearby but also offer interesting, home-cooked food and well-kept ales. Sunday opening times are standard unless specifically mentioned. Pub car parks are available for these walks, provided you are a patron. It would, however, be helpful and courteous if the landlord or a member of staff was made aware that your car was going to be there for the duration of the walk. Some of the pubs are almost on the Coast Path while others are in the nearest village.

The walks are spaced along the coast, some close together, others further apart. With both local and holiday walkers in mind, this grouping makes it possible to undertake several of the walks within a few days before moving on. Walking the Cornwall Coast Path has no rules apart from consideration for the environment and for one's fellows. The walker can quickly escape into a traffic-free zone where only the screaming gulls or the crashing waves disturb the quiet.

In conclusion, the preparation of this book has taken place through winter, spring and summer. I have experienced many glorious, hot, sunny days as well as some gale force winds, mists and rain. The diverse scenery and the company of family and friends have made each walk a special occasion. I hope that you will enjoy our selection of Cornish pubs along the way, and that you, too, will gain as much pleasure as we have done.

Eleanor Smith

WALK 1

MORWENSTOW
The Bush Inn

*This varied walk, about 2 miles south of the county boundary, is based
on the delightful pub in Parson Hawker's Morwenstow and combines a
steep descent and climb – this part of the north coast boasts some of the
highest cliffs in Cornwall, after all – with a sheltered valley, the home of
the rare blue butterfly, where wild daffodils bloom in the spring.*

The Bush Inn, a delightful old thatched pub, dates from the 13th century
and is of monastic origin. It still has a Celtic piscina made of serpentine
stone set in the wall of the kitchen bar and was once a renowned
meeting place for smugglers. As you step into the bar you immediately
feel transported into another age. No modern furnishings or bright lights
but comfortable time-blackened wood and a glowing fire in winter. The
welcome is traditional and genuine, the shining surfaces reflecting the
care that has been lavished on the hostelry over many years.

Meals are only available at lunch-times and these take the form of well-presented and satisfying bar snacks. A ploughman's or home-made soup, sandwiches freshly prepared and generously served or, perhaps, a pie and salad are on offer from Monday to Saturday during the summer and from Tuesday to Saturday during the winter. There is no food on Sunday. This is not to say that you need to go hungry. Just down the road is a farmhouse café which was highly recommended by the landlady of the Bush Inn. Your choice of bar snack may be accompanied by a pint of well-kept Hicks Special or Trelawney Pride from the St Austell Brewery or a draught Guinness, cider or lager. Children are welcome in the pleasant garden.

Opening times are 11.30 am to 3 pm and 7 pm to 11 pm. Closed on Mondays during winter. Telephone: 01288 331242.

- **HOW TO GET THERE:** Turn off the A39 Bideford to Bude road about 3 miles north of Kilkhampton, signed 'Morwenstow'. The pub is just off the road as you enter the village.
- **PARKING:** There is plenty of parking space at the pub.
- **LENGTH OF WALK:** 3 miles. Map: OS Landranger 190 Bude and Clovelly (inn GR 209149).

THE WALK

From the pub join the lane and turn left. Continue until you reach the church, about ¼ mile. You will see the farmhouse café opposite the church. There is also a National Trust map which is interesting as it helps you see the extent of their ownership in this area. Their care is very evident along the stretch of the Coast Path that you are about to walk.

Go through the gate into the churchyard. Bear right, following the yellow arrows and the blue route. You will see curious chimneys on the old vicarage roof. This was once the home of the Rev Robert Stephen Hawker, one of the world's great eccentrics, who arrived in this remote part of Cornwall in 1834. A humorous, compassionate teacher and writer, he is best remembered for his *Song of the Western Men* and the famous *Trelawney*. He wrote much of his work sitting in a tiny hut on the cliff edge which you can visit during this walk.

Go through an attractive area of woodland towards a wooden bridge. Keep straight on, following the yellow arrow waymark, uphill. At a wooden post turn left. Climb a stile and follow the arrow, keeping the hedge on your left. At the next sign leave the blue route and turn left onto the cliffs.

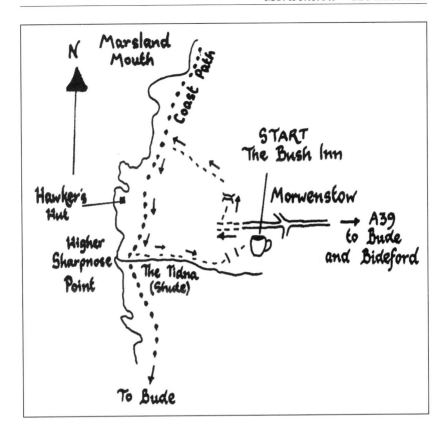

Join the North Cornwall Coast Path. A steep descent now faces you which needs careful walking as it can be slippery. There are interesting rock formations and evidence of contorted strata in the cliffs here. The sedimentary rocks in this area were laid down before the big crumple of 300 million years ago. On reaching valley level cross the bridge and then ascend the cliff ahead by a well-worn path. Go over the stile at the top, still keeping to the cliff edge.

You will soon reach the sign to Hawker's Hut. This hut, now cared for by the National Trust, is built into the cliff and is made from an old boat. The scenery here is spectacular, the isolation in his time would have been complete. Return to the path and walk straight on towards a stile. Over this, you will soon descend some steps into the valley of Tidna Shute.

You will now leave the Coast Path and walk beside a stream up the wooded valley, a host area for many wildflowers, shrubs and the rare

11

blue butterfly. This gradual incline encourages you to walk slowly and enjoy the wildlife away from the harshness of the exposed cliffs. As you reach a white gate bear left, uphill through the wood. At a junction of paths continue straight ahead, following the yellow arrow signs. Do not cross the river. At a wooden post keep to the left – do not go over the stile, but up some steps. Now climb the stile ahead and make for a post and stile across the field opposite. Go over this one, then turn left and over yet another to cross a field and make your way back to the pub.

 ### MARSLAND MOUTH TO PORT ISAAC (33 MILES)

The high cliffs at the start of this north coast stretch reach as far as its first beach at Stanbury Mouth. We then come to an area of Ministry of Defence development, now a satellite tracking station. From Coombe Valley it is possible to walk on sand for 3½ miles to Bude. The coastal path actually follows the clifftop. Bude is famed for its sand and surf and tremendous views can be had from the cliffs above the town, both up and down the coastline. The next 2½ miles to Widemouth offer a series of beach pinnacles until you reach the broad sands at Widemouth. The tiny cove of Millook Haven is a mecca for geologists, the colourful contorted strata in the flanking cliffs attracting enthusiasts from all over the world. The next section has some diverted inland paths due to landslipping. The Coast Path eventually makes its way to Crackington Haven. There are high cliffs here rising to 729 feet, so look for some climbs! On then to Boscastle, that lovely little harbour with houses, shops and inns clustered around the valley. Much of this is National Trust owned.

You now follow an easily recognised path to Tintagel. This well-known place so interwoven with the Arthurian legend is perhaps somewhere to revisit. Climb steeply up to the parish church of St Materiana, prominent on the clifftop. The slate stacks between here and Trebarwith Strand stand lonely on the beach, a haven for gulls and other seabirds. The path continues past Jacket's Point to the one-time fishing village of Port Gaverne. Just around the corner is Port Isaac and the start of our second walk.

PORT ISAAC
The Golden Lion

A *rugged length of coastline with spectacular clifftop scenery between the unspoilt fishing village of Port Isaac and tiny Port Quin, returning over a lane and field paths. The outward route is an exhilarating and energetic tramp involving steep inclines and four flights of steps, two up and two down. An alternative, inland, route is available for those with young children.*

Port Isaac is one of those truly Cornish fishing communities which seems to have remained unchanged and its narrow street leading down to the beach certainly does not encourage much traffic. Set in a sheltered cove, this village has been the scene of many rescues along the rocky shores of Port Isaac Bay. It was a corn port during the 18th century and now boasts an hotel almost on the beach and a collection of interesting shops and restaurants.

The Golden Lion, my chosen pub, was a centre for smuggling activity in the area at one time. Known originally as the Red Lion, it has been an inn since 1716. Horses were stabled in cellars underneath from where there was access to the beach through a tunnel, now blocked, a useful storage place for contraband. The comfortable lounge and eating area where windows look directly out to sea is a fitting place to enjoy locally caught fish and a good Cornish pasty. A real 'local' this with easy conversation and a friendly atmosphere, and children are welcome in the eating area. The menu lists a variety of home-cooked food or snacks such as crab sandwiches or a fisherman's lunch. A choice of mouthwatering sweets is available. A St Austell Brewery house, it serves Tinners, Trelawney and Hicks real ales. Cider and Guinness are on draught. The Bistro, downstairs, is open during the summer months and offers a selection of good wines.

Opening times: Winter 12 noon to 3 pm and 6.30 pm to 11pm; summer 11.30 am to 11 pm. Telephone: 01208 880336.

- **HOW TO GET THERE:** Leave the A39 between Camelford and Wadebridge at the junction with the B3267, signed 'St Teath'. Continue on this road to a crossroads at Pendoggett. Turn left. Take the first right turn, signed 'Port Isaac'. The pub is at the bottom of the steep village street.
- **PARKING:** There is a beach car park adjacent to the pub but it is subject to tidal conditions. It is more convenient to park at the top car park, signed before descending into the village, and walk down.
- **LENGTH OF WALK:** 5½ miles or 3½ miles if you choose the field path route to Port Quin. Map: OS Landranger 200 Newquay and Bodmin (inn GR 995808).

THE WALK

From the pub turn right towards the beach and follow the Coast Path sign on your right. *For the alternative, inland, route to Port Quin*, turn left at the footpath sign as you climb the hill and follow the field paths, all waymarked. *For the cliff walk to Port Quin*, continue up the hill and you will then begin to appreciate the views across the village and coastline. You will soon reach, as promised, the first flight of steps, ascending – I counted 76 so take them steadily. This takes you onto Lobber Point. You will now go downhill to stepping stones and a stile at Pinehaven. A second flight of steps takes you up towards Varley Head. You will walk between fences here and cross two stiles. Some splendid cliff scenery enhances your walk as you reach a seat before the first

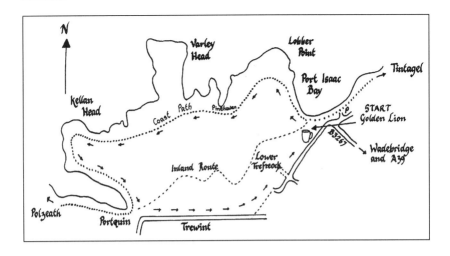

downhill flight of steps. These are very steep so do be careful. Now cross Reedy Cliff and go on to the 'in and out' path around Fox Hole. Shortly afterwards you can take advantage of another seat before descending about 70 steps and walking round Kellan Head. You are now almost at Port Quin and should soon be able to see the folly on Doyden Point. This unusual building, now owned by the National Trust, is let as a holiday home. There is another seat before reaching Port Quin beach, where the Coast Path enters the village.

No doubt you will wish to look around here and notice the conversion of old fish cellars into holiday accommodation. These cellars were used to process the pilchard catch before it was exported to Mediterranean countries to be eaten during Lent. It is said that you could always smell the fishing villages during pilchard harvesting long before you could see them. This peaceful village has just a cluster of houses today, mostly in the care of the National Trust. A rocky beach provides endless enjoyment for children among the pools left by a receding tide. There are no facilities for refreshment here but you will pass a farm on the way back which (in the summer months) offers tea and light meals.

I have chosen to return by the lane and field path route. The lane is quiet and although it begins with a steady climb it soon levels out and makes a change from the strenuous coast walk on the outward journey. Turn left away from the village and continue for about a mile until reaching Trewint Farmhouse where, in summer, you will be able to pause for a drink and snack. Just past this is a footpath sign to the right

15

which you will ignore. Carry on for a few yards to one on the left, signed 'Homer Park'. Cross the stile here and walk straight across the field to the next, visible, stile ahead. Go over this and follow the same line to a high slate stile. Cross this onto a wide track. Immediately opposite is another stile and yellow arrow waymark into a further field. Keeping close to the wall and hedge on your right, make for the bottom of the field and a wooden bridge over a muddy patch. Climb the stile here and cross the stream by a slate bridge where you will pass between two cottages. This is Lower Trefreock and very pretty it is.

Turn right up the lane to a junction and bench. Turn left. Ignore all footpath signs and keep on the lane which becomes Church Hill and leads steeply downhill, back into Port Isaac.

 ### PORT ISAAC TO POLZEATH (7½ MILES)

Follow the Coast Path route from Port Isaac to Port Quin. The subsequent stretch from Port Quin offers the walker some more spectacular scenery. Pass Doyden Point with its folly, now a National Trust holiday cottage, followed by some quite relaxing walking to Rumps Point with its Iron Age cliff castle. On then to Pentire Point and the lovely long, downhill stretch to Hayle Bay at Polzeath. It is difficult to keep one's eyes on the path ahead when the view across the river Camel to Stepper Point opposite claims one's attention. In suitable tidal conditions an easy walk across the beach brings you into Polzeath.

POLZEATH
The Oyster Catcher
❧❀❧

A fine walk for all times of the year. The contrast of a tidal estuary with an inland pastoral scene is not to be missed. Take the opportunity to visit the lovely little church of St Enodoc, where Sir John Betjeman is buried. Once virtually covered by sand, it is now surrounded by a golf course. This is an easy circuit without any stiff climbs or awkward stiles. It is, therefore, suitable for all age groups.

This is a well-known holiday and surfing village, split into two parts, Polzeath and New Polzeath. The bay, shielded on the north by the headland of Pentire Point and to the south by Stepper Point, boasts some fine sands while the Atlantic waves make this a popular place for surfers and a venue for surfing competitions. The sprinkling of shops facing the beach are convenient for holidaymakers who flock here during the summer months. A stream enters the sea across the sand which encourages families of ducks to splash about in the fresh water – an unusual sight on a beach.

The Oyster Catcher, named after that attractive shoreline bird of the north coast, is situated just above the beach, very close to the Coast Path. Originally an hotel, it has been a pub since 1950. The lounge overlooks the sea and Pentire Point with large picture windows to enhance the view. It is a comfortable and spacious place with a happy, welcoming atmosphere. A changing daily blackboard menu offers a choice of seafood dishes along with some local specialities. Sunday lunches are popular while a tasty sandwich or bowl of soup with crusty roll make a good lunchtime snack on any day. There is also a children's menu with their traditional favourites. A St Austell house, it prides itself on well-kept ales – Tinners, Hicks and Trelawney Pride are popular as are Guinness, lagers and cider on draught. A good stock selection of wines is available. You will find a children's room and a pleasant garden area where the youngsters can enjoy themselves.

Opening times: 11 am to 11 pm throughout the summer; 11 am to 3 pm and 6 pm to 11 pm during the winter. Telephone: 01208 862371.

- **HOW TO GET THERE:** Turn off the A39 between Camelford and Wadebridge at the B3267, signed 'St Teath'. At the junction with the B3314 turn left and follow the signs for Polzeath. The pub lies above the beach on the road to Trebetherick and Rock.
- **PARKING:** There is a large car park below the pub. Limited parking in front.
- **LENGTH OF WALK:** 3½ miles. Map: OS Landranger 200 Newquay and Bodmin (inn GR 936788).

THE WALK

From the pub turn left and walk down the hill towards the beach. Pass Tristram car park entrance and continue past a row of cottages to a path on your left, signed 'Coast Path'.

Walk along this path which opens out into open grass and a car park area. Keep left. There are many paths across this headland known as the Greenaway; choose the one that suits you best. The view across to Stepper Point opposite is splendid. As you round Trebetherick Point you will see the sands of Daymer Bay opening up before you, a well-known place for windsurfing. Walk across the car park towards the entrance where there is a shop and toilets. You now leave the Coast Path.

Turn left up the lane and keep going for a few yards until you see a

signpost on your right for St Enodoc church. Go along this enclosed path between houses, over a bridge and onto a golf course. The right of way follows the white stones. **Keep to the path and be wary of golf balls**. It is not necessary to go as far as the church while following this walk but I doubt if many would miss the chance to see this beautiful, isolated building with its leaning steeple. Sir John Betjeman is buried here and his association with this walk is an ever present memory. It was

19

St Enodoc church

while strolling along these paths that many of his poems were conceived and this is a fitting place for his final rest.

If you have followed the stones to the church then retrace your steps towards the little bridge. Before actually reaching it turn right, again following white stones. If you haven't been to the church, after crossing the bridge turn left. The path keeps to the right of some spiny bushes. Keep close to the hedge as the path divides and cross a stile. Walk on, over a bridge, and follow the path through a coppice. Keep on the main path as it wends its way through the trees and enters a field. Turn left. Follow the waymark sign up a sandy track. As the field bends to the right look for a foothpath sign in the hedge on your left with steps down into a lane, a busy one in summer. Turn right and continue uphill for about 100 yards to a public footpath sign on your right. Go along this path, which boasts early violets, until you reach the main road. You are now in Trebetherick. Turn left and pass the lane leading to Daymer Bay. Cross over the main road and in a few yards look for a sign on your right, marked 'Polzeath'. Walk down a track and turn left as the track ends. There is a waymark here into the field. Follow the path along the hedge. At a gap turn right, waymarked, with fine views across the countryside. Keep the hedge on your left at the turn. At the next gate, still keeping the hedge on your left, walk downhill. At the field boundary keep straight on into a wood. A delightful place this with wildflowers according to season. Cross the bridge, climb the stile and walk up a couple of steps. Bear left along a well-trodden path through the trees. On reaching a track turn left, signed 'Polzeath'. Cross over the bridge and go on to Shilla Mill. The track now passes a caravan park and reaches Polzeath opposite the beach. Turn left and follow the road back to the pub.

 ## POLZEATH TO PORTH, NEWQUAY (19½ MILES)

The path from Polzeath follows the river Camel estuary over the Greenaway to Daymer Bay. It is possible to beach walk from here to Rock to catch the ferry to Padstow, but only if the tide is low. The alternative is to walk behind the hill and through the sand dunes, waymarked. After crossing to Padstow you go along the west bank of the river Camel and climb Stepper Point, some 242 feet. There is a 39 foot daymark tower on the top. The cliffs become precipitous for about a mile before gradually sloping down to the sands at Trevone. Harlyn and Mother Ivey's Bay are wide stretches of sand. The lighthouse at Trevose Head comes next and from here the path continues due south. There is an almost continuous line of beaches from here to Porth at Newquay, where our next walk begins.

PORTH, NEWQUAY
The Mermaid Inn

A pleasant circuit, without steep hills. You will enter the pretty village of St Columb Minor and continue along easy tracks through farmland. The section of coastline is quite dramatic with sheer slate cliffs and sandy beaches below. Do go out onto Porth Island across the wooden bridge where, in windy weather, you will see the spray being blown out of the blow hole to cascade onto the springy turf. This walk is suitable for most ages - but take care close to the cliff edge.

Porth is on the northern outskirts of Newquay. It has a superb beach, sheltered by the headland of Trevelgue Head which reaches out to sea, topped by an ancient Iron Age promontory fort. There are tiny coves below and the popular beach area is surrounded by a few shops, houses, hotels and a caravan park. A wide stream enters the sea here creating an environment much enjoyed by young families.

The inn on the beach would be a good name for the pub we have chosen. It began its commercial life as a teashop and has been a pub since the 1950s. By no means a quiet country inn, this lively establishment is suitably managed to cope with its special location. Busy with family groups during the summer, it caters for locals and visitors out of season by offering a comfortable, lively atmosphere in cosy, well-furnished bars. A separate restaurant copes with the influx of customers for a traditional Sunday lunch and for other special occasions. A children's room is also available. With its sea views and easy accessibility to the beach this is, understandably, a much-frequented place.

A varied menu caters for all tastes. For example, there is a good home-made soup with crusty bread while deep fried whitebait or fillet of plaice are two of the fish dishes. A 10 oz rib of beef or a shark steak, a chicken curry or chilli con carne are all really substantial meals. Children's favourites such as fish fingers or jumbo sausage are served with french fries, baked beans or salad. Dutch apple pie or banana longboat are among a choice of sweets. Well-kept ales are a feature of this pub, with Tinners, Trelawney Pride, Guinness and a good mild being among them. Lagers are on draught and there is a good selection of wines.

Opening times are 11 am to 11 pm throughout the year. Food is served until 10.30 pm. Telephone: 01637 872954.

- **HOW TO GET THERE:** Porth lies on the coast road between Newquay and Padstow, the B3276. The pub is situated just alongside Porth beach, about ½ mile from the roundabout junction with the A392 and the A3059 known as Porth Four Turnings.
- **PARKING:** There is ample parking at the pub.
- **LENGTH OF WALK:** 4 miles. Map: OS Landranger 200 Newquay and Bodmin (inn GR 832628).

THE WALK

From the pub car park turn right, cross over and take the first left turn, Lewarne Road. Walk steeply uphill, cross over Green Bank Crescent and continue to the next left turn, Lewarne Crescent. In about 20 yards there is a path on the left. Take this signed route to St Columb Minor. Follow the defined path across the field towards a staggered gate, visible when you reach the brow of the hill. Go through the gate and meet a wide track. Continue along the track, known as Parkenbutts, passing between houses towards the church and village of St Columb Minor. Enter the

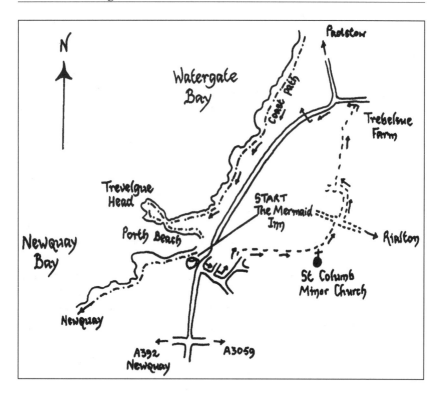

churchyard by a flight of steps on your left. Keep to the right of the church, following a path. You will see twelve trees planted in a row, representing the twelve disciples. Leave the churchyard by a gate onto a track where you turn left.

The track soon becomes a path and makes its way steeply downhill and then up towards a large property on your right. There are splendid views from here across to Porth Island and the beach. Keep left here; do not take the fork marked Rialton. Keep straight on at cross-tracks and walk downhill towards a T-junction. The track bends left here, with a letterbox in the wall. Make for a metal gate ahead. Go through the gate and continue uphill for about ¼ mile towards a farm and buildings. Pass between the buildings. This is Trebelsue Farm. Turn left along a lane which in about 200 yards will join a very busy road. Turn left, taking care and keeping to the wide grass verge. Continue for about 150 yards when you will see, on the opposite side of the road, a fingerpost pointing across a field. Follow this well-marked path towards the coast.

You will join the Coast Path here. Turn left. You now have superb views across not only Watergate Bay below but of the entire Newquay Bay. On reaching two burial barrows walk inland round them. It is thought that these are the graves of prominent members, perhaps kings, of the Dumnoni tribe who inhabited this area during the Bronze Age. The Coast Path is well marked here and well walked. As you continue down towards Porth you will see Trevelgue Head, or Porth Island as it is known locally, reaching out to sea. A defensive position, this Iron Age promontory fort has evidence of banks and ditches to protect it from attack. It is a superb walk around the headland where springy turf and clifftop flowers decorate the steep slate cliffs. A blow hole can be excitingly threatening during a storm or at a very high tide as it appears to explode when the waves crash through the hole created by erosion over thousands of years. You will now see the Mermaid Inn and the beach ahead.

PORTH, NEWQUAY, TO PERRANPORTH (11½ MILES)

The town of Newquay stretches before you. Use the beaches if the tide is low. The river Gannel has to be crossed and there is a ferry service only during the summer. You will need to walk inland to cross by the road bridge at Trevemper and rejoin the Coast Path by turning right along a track high above the Gannel if the tide is really high, otherwise use the footbridge near to Trenance Gardens. The way now proceeds along a lovely path following the river towards Crantock Beach. On then to West Pentire and Porth Joke. The path now rounds Kelsey Head with Cubert Common stretching away to your left. You will probably need to walk the dunes down into Holywell Bay unless the tide is low. Penhale Point is the next headland, from where the path takes you on to Ligger Point and the wide expanse of sand of Perran Beach.

PERRANPORTH
The Seiners Arms

❧❀❧

*A short distance of Coast Path affording magnificent views across
Perran Bay makes a fitting start for this delightful walk. It is an easy
circuit, with field paths and quiet lanes making a strong contrast to the
wild cliff scenery. You will walk along the top of a Cornish hedge – I do
hope you enjoy the experience! A pretty stream and attractive cottages
help to make this 'all the year round' route one of my favourites.*

Perranporth's image of sea, sand and surf is one that attracts
holidaymakers from many parts of the world. Its wide expanse of beach
backed by dunes is the ideal place for associated sports such as surfing
and sand yachting, both enjoyed throughout most of the year. As in
many of Cornwall's coastal villages fishing was the staple industry here
until the late 19th century and mining also had its part to play. The small

town now derives much of its business from the tourist industry but maintains a busy local community.

The Seiners Arms was built early in the 20th century after a fire and bears silent witness to the once thriving seine fishing industry. As many as 18 seine boats were moored in a part of the beach which is still known as 'The Cubby Hole', the old mine shaft in the cliff face being home to nets and sails. A 'huer' or lookout man would patrol the cliffs looking for shoals of pilchards entering the bay. When the cry went up the boats would surround the shoal with their seine nets and the vast quantities of fish would be dragged ashore. Men, women and children would then prepare the catch for home consumption or for export.

Our pub is built on the site of one of the pilchard curing centres. It has been thoroughly and attractively modernised while retaining its link with the past. You will find a large, relaxing bar and a restaurant leading to a garden overlooking the beach, both comfortably furnished and with large windows to enhance the view. The enviable position of the sun terrace brings a continental atmosphere and its white walls, parasols and colourful hanging baskets are a picturesque extension to the bar on warm days. The chef prides himself on the à la carte and table d'hôte menus he serves in the restaurant. The accent is on locally caught fish and traditionally prepared meat dishes. A daily specials board is used in the bar where snacks and meals are served all day. A well-filled crab sandwich or a hearty portion of fish with a generous serving of chips are popular choices, or you might opt for a bowl of tasty soup with a crusty roll. This freehouse serves West Country and Tetley Bitter alongside St Austell Trelawney Pride and Tinners ales. Lagers and Guinness are on draught. Wine is offered by the glass or bottle. Children are welcome.

Opening times are 11.00 am to 12 midnight throughout the year. Telephone: 01872 573118.

- **HOW TO GET THERE:** Directions are given from the A3075 Newquay to Redruth road. Leave the A3075 at Goonhavern and take the B3285, signed 'Perranporth'. Follow signs for the beach. You will arrive at a large car park on your right, adjacent to the beach. The pub lies straight ahead just before the road bends uphill.
- **PARKING:** There is some parking at the pub and a large public car park is nearby.
- **LENGTH OF WALK:** 4 miles. Map: OS Landranger 200 Newquay and Bodmin (inn GR758544).

THE WALK

From the pub turn right up the hill. Walk on to the Coast Path which climbs adjacent to the road after a few yards. Follow the path around the car turning space towards Droskyn Hall. You are now at Droskyn Point. Use the path above the Hall, turning to the right. On approaching the YHA hostel take the acorn sign and follow the wall. Do not leave the path along the wall but keep left of capped mine shafts to a stile in the wall. Turn left away from the sea, keeping along the wall. You now leave the Coast Path.

On reaching some houses go over the stile and onto a track. At the road turn right and cross over carefully. Just past the last bungalow on the left there is a track and waymark post, signed 'Perrancoombe'. Go down this lovely old track, ignoring a stile on your left and another on the right. Continue on the track. It soon narrows and passes through woodland. You will reach some houses and a stream when the path ends. Turn right over the bridge and join a lane. Turn left and cross over. You are in Perrancoombe.

You will now need to look for a house called Magpies with an iron gate immediately past it. At the time of writing there was no waymark post here. Turn right, through the gate, and join an uphill track leading to a stile. As you reach the top of the hill you will enjoy views across Perranporth. You will also see a caravan site ahead.

Keeping the hedge on your left, make for a gap ahead and climb the steps to the left of the caravans. This is where you walk on the Cornish hedge. These substantial protective boundary hedges are stone built and infilled with soil. Seeds germinate and plants grow, thus making an effective dense barrier between fields.

On reaching a busy road, turn right. There are wide verges but care is needed. The road winds uphill. Cross over before reaching the brow in about ¼ mile where you will join a path. Take the footpath sign on the left, 'Polglaze Farm'. Cross some waste ground and walk to the right of a bungalow along a track. The route now continues along this track until you reach a stile on the right. Climb the stile and join a very pretty sunken path lined with moss and wildflowers. It can be somewhat slippery down here after wet weather. On reaching the end of the path climb a stile leading into a lane. You are now in Penwartha Coombe.

This attractive village of cottages and houses has a stream running beside the lane. Look for the mill with its wheel still in situ on your right. You will soon reach the village of Bolingey. Pass the village inn on your left. Take the next left turn where you will pass a superbly thatched

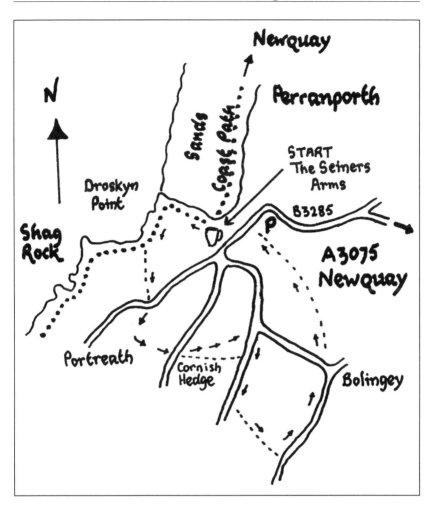

cottage. At the speed de-restriction sign turn right along a wide track. The route now follows this to a grass-covered island where there is a fork. Do not go uphill here but keep straight ahead. Continue to follow the same line at the next fork, keeping straight on towards some houses. As you join a lane, turn left.

Leave the lane at the first left-hand path, waymarked, using the lower of the two paths. On reaching a road cross over and pass between a development of flats. Keep straight ahead over the next road, walking between shops to the main street. Turn left and then right and so back to the pub.

PERRANPORTH TO PORTREATH (11½ MILES)

Follow the pub walk directions until you pass Droskyn Point. The Cornwall Coast Path then continues to Cligga Head. Here can be seen the results of former mining activity in profusion. Following this period of industry a dynamite factory was built here which, although closed down and demolished many years ago, has added its remnants to the scarred landscape of this superb coastal route. The path descends steeply into Trevellas Coombe and on to Trevaunance Combe, the beach for St Agnes. Follow the cliff around Newdowns Head to St Agnes Head where you look above the cliffs, inland, to St Agnes Beacon which rises to 628 feet.

The route now follows a clear path towards Chapel Porth, passing the engine house of Wheal Coates restored by the National Trust. On to Chapel Porth, also owned by the Trust, where you will find toilets and, during the summer, refreshments. You will now climb the southern headland and join the cliff path towards Porthtowan. The next section, beyond Porthtowan beach, goes on the seaward side of a Government Research Station. Fenced with high wire it has gates at intervals which can be used to close the coastal path if necessary. However this prerogative is rarely used. Notices in both Porthtowan and Portreath are displayed if this is likely. On reaching Portreath enter the village by passing the white daymark known as the Pepper Pot.

PORTREATH
The Basset Arms
❧❀❧

This fine walk includes splendid cliff scenery then a stroll through Tehidy Country Park. Choice woodlands, drifts of springtime bluebells, rhododendrons, a variety of shrubs and easily walked paths make this lovely area a pleasure to enter. Before wandering down 'Primrose Valley' back into Portreath under the old Incline bridge you are very likely to enjoy a friendly encounter with some of the birds and animals of Duchy Farm College. This is a varied, interesting route. The steep bits on the cliff path (there are some helpful steps) are rewarded by the panoramic views. Keep children away from the edge!

Portreath has a fascinating history as a fishing and mineral port and some evidence of this is still visible today, for example, the remains of the 1809 Tram Road to St Day, thought to be the first railway in Cornwall, and the remarkable Incline Shaft of 1838, which pulled trucks of coal up the steep hill opposite the harbour. Portreath has long been the 'seaside'

to the towns of Redruth and Camborne. Today people come here from further away too. Surfing is popular but there is room enough for buckets and spades as well. The Basset family, from which our pub takes its name, were distinguished mineral lords who lived in the mansion at nearby Tehidy, set in the beautiful grounds through which this walk passes.

The Basset Arms is a freehouse and family owned. It more than justifies its reputation as a good place to eat. Basset's Pantry, as the restaurant is known, is spacious and comfortably furnished. The menu offers variety while the service is friendly and efficient. Bar meals include well-named 'doorstep' sandwiches with a choice of fillings. Crab or prawn salads are popular while vegetarians can order a tikka masala or a potato, cheese and leek pie. Steaks form an important part of the menu and the desserts include some delicious speciality ice creams. It is as well to reserve a table for the popular Sunday lunch. Well-kept beers, which include Tetley, Bass, Dartmoor and Kilkenny bitters, are served and Strongbow cider, various lagers and an extensive wine list are also available. There is a play area for children and garden seating for sunny days.

Opening times: 11 am to 11 pm during the summer, 11 am to 2.30 pm and 6 pm to 11 pm in winter. Sunday opening hours are 12 noon to 3 pm and 6.30 pm to 10.30 pm. Telephone: 01209 842077.

- **HOW TO GET THERE:** Directions are given from Redruth. Leave the town by the bypass, taking the well-signed B3300 for Portreath. On reaching the village continue towards the beach car park. Leaving that car park on your right the road bends sharply to the left. The entrance to the pub car park is immediately on your left.
- **PARKING:** Should the pub car park be full it will be necessary for you to use the pay and display beach park.
- **LENGTH OF WALK:** 4 miles. Map: OS Landranger 203 Land's End and The Lizard (inn GR 656455).

THE WALK

From the pub car park walk out onto the road. Cross carefully here to the road opposite, Battery Hill. The route follows this roadway until it bends right to a small cove. You will see a Coast Path sign here. Follow it, walking up the hill. At the top keep to the left-hand path when you reach the cliff edge. Take care here although the path is wide and well used. Walk onto the open clifftops with a magnificent panorama

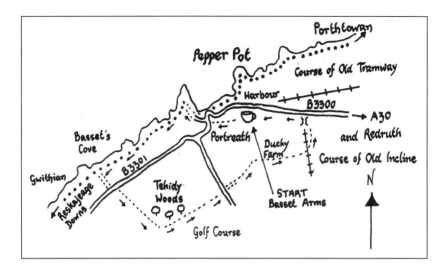

and a wealth of wildflowers, particularly in early June. In about ¼ mile you will arrive at a steep descent. Follow marker signs which take you on a zig-zag course. Be sure you keep right as the path bends sharply. Follow the gravel path all the way down. At the bottom is a wooden bridge which you cross before ascending by a clearly marked path. Steps help on this climb. In a short distance the path descends again by granite-faced steps. Climb the next hill, keeping close to the left-hand fence. The route now goes slightly inland and then bears right towards a stile and a car park above Basset's Cove, National Trust. Leave the Coast Path here.

Turn left, taking the footpath alongside the wide track until reaching a road. Turn left, cross over and walk a few yards to a footpath sign on your right. Cross a grid to join an enclosed path into Tehidy Woods. On reaching a junction of four paths keep straight ahead, the second exit path from the left, continuing on the main track. Ignore all side paths, including one wide track on the left, signed 'Pedestrians Only'. On reaching a wooden perimeter fence turn left and keep straight on with the fence on your right. You will soon reach a wooden sign where you take the track signed to East Lodge.

The route now skirts a golf course with superb views across to Carn Brea and its eye-catching monument to Lord de Dunstanville, a member of the Basset family. Continue until the track forks and there is a wooden seat. Turn right through a gate, over a grassed area, then through another gate to join the Pine Walk. This new plantation replaces an old established avenue of pine trees which were evidently felled some years ago. Continue on this main track to a lodge. Turn left onto a busy road.

Cross over and walk beneath a canopy of overhanging trees for about 200 yards. On reaching a wide track on your right with a sign, 'No Tipping', turn right along the track. Walk along this pretty path which bends left then right and continues for about ½ mile. After passing through a metal gate ignore the grid on the right and continue via a rather muddy patch of ground towards some wooden chalets on the left. You are now almost at the Duchy College Farm buildings. Here you will probably be greeted by guinea fowl and ducks. Other animals and birds are in pens around you. Follow the footpath signs through the farm buildings and join an enclosed path. Turn left at the first side track towards a pond. Go down some steps into a lovely valley. Keep on the track with a stream on your left down to a castellated house known as Glenfeadon Castle. Turn left at the lane and pass under the Incline bridge. This was in continuous use for about 100 years until 1930 when road transport took over. Turn into a narrow lane fronting a row of cottages and continue along here until reaching the pub.

 ### Portreath to St Ives (16 miles)

Follow the pub walk as far as the car park above Basset's Cove. This particularly fine stretch of the Coast Path reaches a height of 200 feet. The path runs close to the cliff edge in places and care should be taken, particularly during wet weather. As the cliffs open up onto Reskajeage Downs it becomes much safer. At Hell's Mouth the path, road and cliff edge all come together where there is a vertical drop of 200 feet to the sea below. The road and path now part once again and the route follows an arm of land out to Godrevy Point. Godrevy Island with its well-known lighthouse atop presents a spectacular scene. Wide views across St Ives Bay make for a pleasurable walk over Upton Towans. On the approach to Hayle it is possible to cross the harbour by a bridge but it is then necessary to follow the main road through the town, making for Lelant. Some maps may still show a ferry here but to the best of my knowledge there has not been one for many years. Rejoin the Coast Path at Lelant church where a pleasant, scenic walk above Porth Kidney Sands followed by Carbis Bay brings you to Porthminster Point and on to St Ives itself. Walk 7 joins the Coast Path at Porthmeor Beach.

ST IVES
The Croft

❦

*I*t is quite surprising how quickly one can leave the bustling jumble of
St Ives town and walk almost in solitude over an impressive headland
and along a well-signed path. This relatively short walk includes a
variety of terrain, some road walking and the minimum of climbs. There
is not a single stile!

St Ives has had so much written about it that most people visiting
Cornwall feel that they already know it without even having been there
– its narrow streets, its beaches, the pasties and saffron cake, the
fishermen's cottages packed closely together up the slope from the
harbour, the new museum and the distinctive atmosphere generated by
the artists and potters who have made their home here for decades. It
may well be tourist orientated these days but nothing can take away the
truly Cornish feel of this attractive little town.

Park and ride facilities have solved some of the problems of access for people visiting St Ives, but I have been lucky enough to have found a pub very close to the Coast Path with a large car park. Not only does the Croft have a car park but it also serves good food in a pleasant, friendly atmosphere and has a beer garden and adequate space for children to play. A large council maintained playground is just across the road, which is an added attraction. This is a family run pub with good home-cooking and well-kept ales. What more could we want?

The beers include Flowers IPA, Boddingtons and Marston's Pedigree, all from the cask. Stella Artois and Heineken lager are on draught as are Guinness and Strongbow cider. There is a choice of popular wines. Traditional menus using freshly-cooked local produce, when available, are served all day, alongside a daily 'special'.

Opening times: 9 am to 11 pm during the summer, 12 noon to 3 pm and 7 pm to 11 pm in the winter. Telephone: 01736 797473.

- **HOW TO GET THERE:** From the A30 between Penzance and Redruth take the A3074 from the roundabout at Lelant. Do not continue on the A3074 to St Ives but take the first left turn onto a minor road, signed 'Trencrom'. At the next fork keep right, do not go up to Trencrom but pass Bowl Rock on your right in about ½ mile. On reaching the B3311 turn right, signed 'St Ives'. At the junction with the B3306, turn right. You will pass a filling station on your left and the pub is almost opposite on the right.
- **PARKING:** There is plenty of parking at the pub.
- **LENGTH OF WALK:** 3½ miles. Map: OS Landranger 203 Land's End and The Lizard (inn GR 515404).

THE WALK

Turn right out of the car park and right again onto the main road. Walk past the Leach Pottery and continue down the hill towards the town centre and the sea. Make for the harbour, where, no doubt, you will have your own ideas about what to see in St Ives. The colourwashed cottages and closely packed shops in the narrow streets seem to entice you in all directions at once. However, our route joins the Cornwall Coast Path just above Porthmeor Beach, so follow signs for that beach.

Walk through the car park to the far side where you will see a flight of steps. Halfway up these, turn right onto a tarmac path, in fact the Coast Path. Stretching ahead of you is Clodgy Point, a lovely place to relax, with its spray washed turf and rocky outcrop reaching out to sea.

Continue to follow the path and bear left at the acorn sign. You will

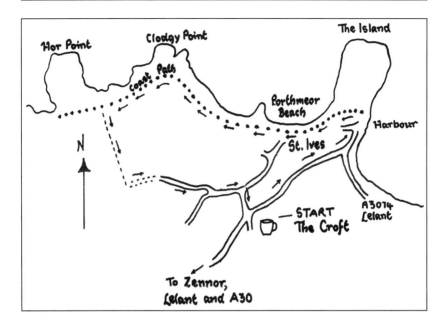

shortly see a stone inscribed 'Zennor 6½ miles'. Go through a gap in the wall and then walk straight on towards a seat on the headland. This short detour is well worth the few extra steps to appreciate the splendid view. To continue, bear left through the gap and make your way uphill, straight ahead. In about ½ mile and after a right-hand bend there is a boggy patch followed by an uphill track. You will now come to a Coast Path sign.

This is where you leave the Coast Path and walk straight on, following a made up path, uphill. On reaching a farmhouse on your right keep straight ahead, following a yellow arrow sign. As you reach a wide track turn left. The track soon becomes metalled and passes some houses. At the road junction, turn left then right and continue on the pavement to a junction. Cross over where you will see the pub across the road.

 ### ST IVES TO PENDEEN (11½ MILES)

The Coast Path from St Ives to Pendeen is somewhat rough in places. Follow the pub walk from Porthmeor Beach to beyond Clodgy Point then continue through the National Trust ground at Hor Point. Between Carn Naun Point and Mussel Point lie the Carracks where you just may be lucky enough to see some seals. On then to Zennor Head, National

Trust, where you may well go inland for a visit to the Tinners Arms for food and drink. Gurnard's Head is the next headland with its Iron Age promontory fort, worth a separate visit perhaps. On then to Greeb Point from where you will see the impressive white column of Pendeen Watch.

PENDEEN
The Radjel Inn
❦

*D*iverse scenery, a spectacular lighthouse, granite stiles and lots to interest the industrial archaeology enthusiast! This section of the North Cornwall Coast Path is now showing signs of the area's reclamation from its mining past and is a typical walk for the far west corner of the county.

Pendeen, a large village situated in the heart of the mining district of far west Cornwall, is very close to Geevor mine. One of the last mines to close, this thriving enterprise extracted thousands of tons of tin and provided employment for most of the men living in and around the area. However, those days have gone and the busy work place is now a heritage centre, a fascinating enterprise where one can get some idea of life in this part of the county over past generations. Pendeen is still a busy village. Interesting shops and friendly people make this a good place from which to begin a very special walk that is steeped in history.

The name Radjel is very rare indeed. As the pub is situated in the middle of a mining community one would, perhaps, expect its name to relate to that industry. Not so. Radjel is the name given to a fox's lair when, instead of being a hole in the ground, it is made within a pile of stones. The attractive sign illustrates this very well. The pub began life as three cottages and is thought to have become an inn about 1900. It is comfortably furnished with a warm, spacious lounge bar and a small public bar with a cheerful open fire in winter. This family run village inn serves a good selection of St Austell ales, Hicks, Bosun's, Tinners and Trelawney Pride. These well-kept brews are to be found alongside a mild ale, with Murphy's and Guinness on draught, as well as lagers and a choice of wines. Good, home-cooked food is offered on a menu which should suit most tastes and appetites. A firm favourite is haddock smokie, smoked fish in a cheese sauce with chips or crusty bread. Another light meal is pizza with chips or salad while a jumbo sausage is a real filler. For the more serious diner a sirloin steak or hot chilli, gammon or chicken make a hearty meal. Snacks include freshly-made soup, a choice of sandwiches and rolls and ploughman's lunches served with either cheese, ham, smoked mackerel or crab. Children are welcome in the games room and garden.

Opening times: Monday to Saturday all day throughout the year, Sunday 12 noon to 3 pm and 7 pm to 10.30 pm. Telephone: 01736 788446.

- **HOW TO GET THERE:** Pendeen lies on the scenic coast road between St Ives and St Just, the B3306. The pub is in the centre of the village.
- **PARKING:** There is a large car park at the pub and a public one within about 200 yards.
- **LENGTH OF WALK:** 5½ miles. Map: OS Landranger 203 Land's End and The Lizard (inn GR 383343).

THE WALK

From the pub car park the route turns right towards the village shop. Take the first right turn, signed to the lighthouse, which is just one mile from here. On reaching a T-junction turn left. As you approach the lighthouse, known as Pendeen Watch, just opposite a house on the right and before a white signboard on your left, there is a Coast Path sign set in a granite boulder.

Join the Coast Path here. Walk along the clearly defined path for about ½ mile until reaching Geevor mine where you descend and

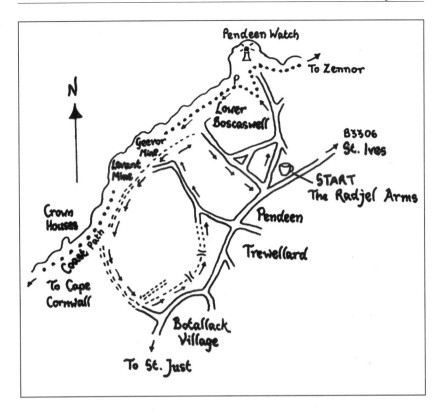

then bear left until you reach a pool on your left where the path turns right. There may be minor changes to the route as the museum site develops but it is well signposted. Keep straight on between mine buildings until you reach Levant mine engine house. Now owned by the National Trust, it is open to the public occasionally. The peaceful scene of today gives little indication of the tragedy which occurred here in 1919 when a cap on the engine above ground snapped and 31 men hurtled to their death below.

Continue along the wide track, keeping straight along the coast. The Path follows closely, a spectacular walk but rather rough. It is very much easier to keep to the wide track just inland. In about a mile, after passing a recently modernised house on your left, you will enter the Botallack mining area. This is where the famous Crown Houses are located on ledges just above sea level. At the turn of the century it was possible to pay a small charge and descend into this mine, which ran under the sea bed. Queen Victoria and Prince Albert came here, the Prince

41

descending into the mine. It is much visited today by artists and photographers. You now leave the Coast Path.

Turn inland along the wide track, passing a large house, a bungalow and then a farmhouse on your left. Immediately past the track leading to the farm buildings there is a path. Take this and join a track beside the buildings. Walk along the track for about 100 yards and look for a granite stile on your right. Go over this and then the next visible one close to some large boulders. Now walk diagonally across the field towards a metal gate. Go through this and turn left, over a stile. Follow the track, which soon becomes a path. Keep to this path round the field with the hedge on your right. Look for a step stile on your right. Climb the steps and go over the stile. Turn left and walk towards a granite stile ahead. Go over this, now keeping alongside a low hedge on your left. You will now reach a rather dilapidated wooden stile. Climb this and follow the wooden fence on your right for a few yards to a granite stile, the last one, and on to a track. Turn right. Continue on the track, which widens into a lane, and reach a T-junction alongside a house. There is a convenient bench here.

The village to your right is Trewellard. Turn left, seawards. Walk down the lane, ignoring all waymarked tracks until you reach Levant mine again where you will rejoin the Coast Path.

On reaching the pool in Geevor mine turn right and follow a marked path uphill where you keep to the left and join a track leaving the works area. The track then continues past some bungalows on your left. On reaching the road turn right and continue through the village of Lower Boscaswell until you reach the coast road. Turn left and you will see the pub ahead.

 ### PENDEEN WATCH TO TREEN (14 MILES)

From the Coast Path south of Pendeen Watch follow the pub walk as far as Botallack mine. The coastline is now running almost north to south. The next headland, Cape Cornwall, the only cape in England, looms ahead with the offshore reef known as the Brisons. The path passes an interesting barrow at Carn Gloose. After Aire Point the sands of Whitesand Bay can be followed, tide permitting. The path keeps closely to the coastline on gently sloping cliffs. From Sennen Cove the route goes up to Maen Castle fort and continues on open cliffs for nearly one mile to Land's End, developed and touristy but still a place of pilgrimage. There is no charge for the walker. We now turn the corner of western

England and take the Coast Path south-eastwards past Enys Dodman and the Armed Knight. There is a magnificent cliff line to the village of Porthgwarra. Here it becomes more gentle as we approach St Levan and the Minack Theatre at Porthcurno, hewn out of the cliffside more than 200 feet above the sea, and continue along the Coast Path to join Walk 9 as far as Penberth Cove south-east of Treen.

TREEN
The Logan Rock Inn
❧

This walk incorporates some of the most dramatic scenery along the Cornish Coast Path as well as an opportunity to see the famous Logan Rock and a detour to visit the spectacular cliffside Minack Theatre. Golden sands and the often turquoise sea of Porthcurno beach add to the attraction of this circuit as does the total contrast of secluded Penberth Cove with its workaday atmosphere of fishing boats and capstan wheel. A route of variety and interest for everyone except very young children.

According to local legend tin streamers of long ago brought their produce to this village to trade with Phoenician merchants who came to the nearby cove of Penberth in their boats. Today, Treen is better known as the village from which the footpath to the Logan Rock runs. Logan or logging (rocking) occurs from the result of weathering – the slightest touch would set it rocking. In 1824 a young lieutenant, encouraged by a group of high-spirited naval officers, levered it out of position. Such was the fuss made by local inhabitants that the Admiralty were forced to replace it as near as possible to its original location. The cost of £130 was borne by the unfortunate lieutenant.

This old and unspoilt hostelry displays all its original charm and character. It is known to have been an inn since 1900 and one can be assured of a warm welcome from the landlord and staff. A St Austell Brewery house, it serves their draught and bottled beers. A local favourite is Hicks Special Draught. Tinners Ale is another popular brew. Guinness, lager and cider are also on draught and there is a good selection of wines. Food is on offer here all the year round. Some dishes have local names, such as Logan Rock Seafarer which is an unusual layered combination of fish and sliced green beans with onion and tomato sauce topped with breadcrumbs and cheese crumble, served with a green salad. Because of the proximity to Porthcurno and the Minack Theatre another dish is called Minack Melody. Steaks, basket meals, jacket potatoes, and sandwiches are all generous and a children's menu offers their usual favourites. Desserts come with clotted cream. Tea and coffee are available at all times.

Opening times: Monday to Saturday 10.30 am to 11 pm from May to September, 11 am to 3 pm and 5 pm to 11 pm in the winter months. Sunday opening is from 12 noon to 3 pm and 7 pm to 10.30 pm. Food is served on Monday to Saturday from 12 noon to 9 pm between June and September and from 12 noon to 2 pm and 7 pm to 9 pm between October and May. On Sundays it is available from 12 noon to 2.30 pm and 7 pm to 9 pm. Telephone: 01736 810495.

- **HOW TO GET THERE:** Directions are given from Penzance. Leave by the A30 Land's End road. In about 3 miles at Catchall turn left onto the B3283. Continue on this road (which changes to the B3315) for approximately 5 miles and you will see the Logan Rock Inn sign on your left just past the turning to Penberth.
- **PARKING:** There is a car park at the pub and a public park a few yards away.
- **LENGTH OF WALK:** 4 miles or 5 miles if you detour to look at the Minack Theatre. Map: OS Landranger 203 Land's End and The Lizard (inn GR 394231).

THE WALK

From the pub turn right then take the track on the right opposite Corner

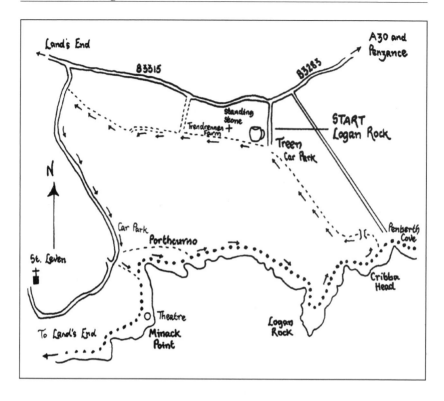

Cottage and in front of Houses Farm. Bear right to the gate, beside which is a stile and waymark arrow. The path follows the left-hand hedge to a gap. Make for the next stile, adjacent to a gate. Notice the standing stone on your right, probably an old waymark. Make for a gate and stile, following the left-hand hedge. Cross to the next facing stile. Continue straight ahead towards the farmhouse of Trendrennen and cross the next stile in the hedge. Keep to the right-hand wall and enjoy the views across to the cliffs and sea. Climb a stile into the yard and turn left, waymarked. The route now turns right and passes in front of a row of cottages. Continue to the metal gate ahead. Go through this and bear left along a wide track. As the track turns left and stops at a gate keep straight on. I found it necessary to keep to the left-hand hedge here as the field was cropped. You will reach a stile in the hedge with a metal post but no sign. Climb this and turn right along the hedge towards the road where there is a gate and stile. Turn left onto a footpath.

Continue down the road, carefully when the footpath ends, and walk through the small village. You will soon pass the old Cable and Wireless college on your left before reaching the beach car park. Turn left into the car park which you will cross diagonally left towards a sign to the beach. Continue on the track until just before a National Trust sign, 'Porthcurno'. A detour of 1 mile to visit the Minack Theatre is possible by turning right along the Coast Path at this point. This theatre on the cliff edge is well signed and can be viewed whenever a performance is not taking place. To continue the walk, turn left up an unmarked path through trees. For those who don't mind a stiff climb do not take this path but continue a little further towards the beach where you will see the Coast Path sign to Penberth. These two paths join.

 The Coast Path is well trodden and easily followed except for the initial climb. At a fork keep to the higher path. Continue on the path until you reach a National Trust sign, 'Logan Rock'. You can detour here to view the stone or just enjoy the magnificent scenery. The path passes behind a grassy hillock and continues to Penberth Cove. This is a particularly spectacular stretch of the Coast Path. It is a steep and rather rough descent into the cove but improves after the first few yards. Steps have been cut lower down. This beautiful cove is National Trust owned and the cottages are let to local people. Fishing boats, a capstan to haul the boats from the water, even the scales for weighing the catch are all there.

Leave the Coast Path here and turn left. Pass in front of the group of cottages and look for a path on your left which passes over a clapper bridge. Cross this, turn right and walk in front of a house on your left. Continue through a wooden gate and join an enclosed path. At a fork turn left where you will probably find a boggy area as you walk uphill. You will eventually reach a steep stile. Go over this into a meadow. Keep straight ahead to the next stile. Cross this, and, keeping the same line, make for another step stile, rather obscure in high summer. Go over this into the next field where you will bear left to the next visible stile. Climb this into the field adjacent to the public car park at Treen. Turn right and so back to the pub.

TREEN TO PERRANUTHNOE (17½ MILES)

After Penberth Cove the first 3 or 4 miles pass through secluded country as the cliff scenery becomes more gentle and lush. St Loy is said to be one of the warmest places in Britain. Pass Tater-du lighthouse whose mournful note bleats forth during fog. Pass the 'Silent Cross of Lamorna', a granite cross about 5 feet high with no name and no inscription, a

The beautiful cove of Penberth, owned by the National Trust

silent, touching memorial to someone or something. Lamorna Cove with its cluster of cottages and its pub, the Wink, just up the road, leads on to the next stretch of coast and to the picturesque village of Mousehole before joining the promenade past Newlyn into Penzance. The route now continues close to the railway line to Marazion and the imposing structure of St Michael's Mount some 500 yards offshore. Walk on along the coast to Perran Sands below Perranuthnoe.

PERRANUTHNOE
The Victoria Inn

This scenic walk covers a variety of terrain. The low cliffs make for easy walking along the Coast Path and the interesting coves of Prussia, Bessy's and Piskies are a delight, as are the attractive buildings en route. Inland the paths are lush especially during high summer. A pleasant circuit, no steep climbs, a few stiles and some superb views, particularly of St Michael's Mount.

The village of Perranuthnoe is picturesquely set on a hillside above a low cliff with Perran Sands below, a good, sandy beach at low tide. Its view of the dominating St Michael's Mount, to the west, is that of a rocky outline, very different from the village area shown to Marazion.

The Victoria Inn is thought to have been built during the 12th century as a hostelry for the masons working on the village church. It also lays claim to being the oldest inn in Cornwall. With a long history such as this there are many tales to be told - for example, of the years when criminals being taken from the Land's End area to Bodmin gaol rested in the cellar here overnight. Present day travellers enjoy the inn's privileged position so close to the beach and Coast Path while its cellar now contains liquid refreshment rather than prisoners.

This is an Ushers house and prize-winning Spring Fever and Best Bitter are among the well-kept brews served. The usual lagers are available as are a selection of wines. The menu is updated each day with 'specials'. Locally caught fish is always popular, especially when served with a delicious salad, and the generous sandwiches are freshly prepared. Vegetarian dishes are tasty and include a lasagne or perhaps a curry. A family room caters for children, and old favourites such as sausage, beans and chips or fish fingers are among the meals offered to them.

Opening times are 11 am to 11 pm during the summer, 11 am to 3 pm and 6 pm to 11 pm in the winter. Telephone: 01736 710309.

- **HOW TO GET THERE:** Turn off the Penzance to Helston road, the A394, about 4 miles east of Penzance. On reaching Perranuthnoe the pink-colourwashed inn is on your left.
- **PARKING:** There is adequate parking at the pub.
- **LENGTH OF WALK:** 4½ miles. Map: OS Landranger 203 Land's End and The Lizard (inn GR 538296).

THE WALK

From the pub turn left then left again. Turn right at the T-junction and follow the road down towards the beach. Look for a Coast Path sign on the left as you approach the beach and walk along the tarmac driveway.

Continue until reaching a fork, then turn right, signed but possibly rather overgrown. Turn left as you approach beach level, the sign is in the hedge. Look ahead to Cudden Point. Cross two fields on a well-defined path, keeping close to the right-hand hedge. Climb a high stile and look back at St Michael's Mount and Mount's Bay. Stay on the right as the path forks, keeping close to the cliff edge, although the path straight ahead looks tempting! Keep left at the next Coast Path sign in about 20 yards. Acton Castle now comes into view.

Cross a bridge and another stile. Go over two more and another bridge and you will come to the National Trust sign at Cudden Point. You can walk out onto the point if you wish but the views from this spot are superb, especially of the Mount, the Lizard peninsula and the Goonhilly Earth Station. A remote house stands, solitary, on your left. As

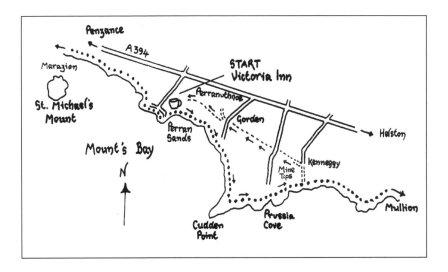

the paths divide the Coast Path actually goes close to the cliff edge but I kept to the left and approached Prussia Cove. There are interesting old buildings here, particularly an ancient thatched cottage now used as a store. Keep to the upper path in the cove, which soon becomes a track and is signed. Turn right at a track junction, signed. Using a stile if the gate is closed, pass between two houses. Cross a stream and pass some cottages on the left.

At a signpost, without a sign, bear left uphill and leave the Coast Path. You will see evidence of mining here. Keep right, passing a burnt-out building on the left, and join a track which narrows to a path. Keep straight on when it becomes a track again and approaches some houses (Kenneggy). At Sunnyvale Farm leave the road and turn left along a track. Ignore side tracks. As the track bends to the left into a field follow it – do not continue on the obvious footpath ahead. Keep to the defined path across fields and drop down to reach two wooden gates leading to a road. Turn right, then almost immediately left along a signed path. This enclosed path leads into fields with an opening to the right and straight ahead. Take the straight-on route, keeping to the right-hand hedge. Walk slowly here, particularly in high summer, as the step stile in the right-hand hedge can become overgrown. It is located almost opposite an iron gate leading into a field on the left. You may well think you are trespassing here as you climb the stile into a carefully tended commercial garden. However it is a right of way.

Keep closely to the left hedge on a well-defined path and leave the garden by a stile onto a road. Turn left. Almost immediately turn right along a track. In about 100 yards you will see a stile and footpath sign on your left. Go over this into the field and follow the right-hand hedge until you see a stile in the next hedge, diagonally left. Go over this. Now keep to the left-hand hedge in the next field to another stone stile. Cross this and turn right, making your way towards a farmhouse. Go over the stile. You are at the hamlet of Treen. Turn left alongside the buildings and bear right to a footpath sign on the left. Follow the path, which becomes enclosed. On entering an open field keep straight ahead and walk immediately in front of a row of houses. The path enters Perranuthnoe opposite the pub.

 PERRANUTHNOE TO MULLION (12½ MILES)

The cliff paths are low and relatively easy along this section and include some long stretches of sandy beaches at Perran Sands and Praa Sands. Prussia Cove was once a notorious smugglers' retreat. There is a ruined outline of a 16th-century castle at Pengersick, which is followed by the last of the granite outcrops at Rinsey and Trewavas Heads. The harbour at Porthleven and the long stretch of sands passing Loe Pool lead on to Gunwalloe. Stories of shipwrecked treasure here have been credible enough for searches to have been made. However, nobody has been lucky enough to find real treasure. Pass the Marconi Memorial, which marks the first transatlantic wireless transmission in 1901. On to Polurrian Cove and then to Mullion Cove, following the route of Walk 11.

MULLION
The Old Inn

The Lizard area has a wild and rugged coastline with tremendous gorges cut into the colourful serpentine rock over thousands of years. This walk passes along some magnificent cliff formations, but with Mullion Cliff providing the only really steep climb, then moves inland over gentle farm tracks, going close to an ancient Cornish cross, probably used as a waymark generations ago.

Mullion has much to commend it – a very pretty village and its position at the western gateway of some of the grandest coastal scenery in Britain. The sun rides higher here than anywhere else in the country while Atlantic gales can lash the shores or sea mists lend their mystery to this spectacular part of Cornwall.

The Old Inn, dating from the 16th century, is situated on the Poldhu road out of the village and occupies a delightful spot with a mature garden equipped with chairs and tables for outdoor summer meals. Its decor reflects all aspects of life in this coastal location. Nets and nautical brasses, pictures and photographs of incidents along the treacherous shoreline claim your interest as you wait for a drink or meal. There are low beams and comfortable benches in the bar while a spacious dining room caters for main meals. This is a Greenalls house serving Bass, Wadworth 6X and Flowers IPA real ales. Guinness and lagers are on draught and a selection of wines is available. Fish features prominently on the menu – and a fresh local crab salad is something to be remembered. There is a choice of fillings for the generously served granary bread sandwiches and the daily 'specials' are always popular. Children are welcome in the dining room and garden.

Opening times are 11 am to 3 pm and 6 pm to 11 pm. The inn is open all day on Saturday and Sunday and throughout the summer months. Food orders are taken from 12 noon to 2 pm and 6 pm to 9 pm. Telephone: 01326 240240.

• **HOW TO GET THERE:** Turn off the A3083 between Helston and the Lizard at Cross Lanes, south of RNAS Culdrose. In about 2 miles you will arrive at Mullion village (not the cove). Turn right towards the church. The pub is just past the church on the left.

• **PARKING:** There is some parking at the pub and a public car park nearby.

• **LENGTH OF WALK:** 3½ miles. Map: OS Landranger 203 Land's End and The Lizard (inn GR 678193).

THE WALK

From the Old Inn turn right towards the village. In about 10 yards look for a footpath sign on your right, signed 'Polurrian'. Take this path which passes a playing field and then enters a bungalow estate. Cross over at the T-junction and follow the continuing path opposite. This path finishes with steps onto a lane. Bear left down a gravelled path past some cottages. At a fork take the left-hand track, signed 'To the Beach'. This pretty path soon opens up to give superb views of Polurrian Cove. Cross over a wooden bridge on your left as you reach the cove and join the Coast Path.

Climb steps up the cliff. It soon levels out along a track where you pass under a wooden bridge. On joining a lane turn right, following the Coast Path sign. Join a tarmac drive for a few yards, then keep right along a path. There is a National Trust plaque here signed 'Polurrian'. In early summer the cliff edge is covered in a variety of wildflowers, thrift,

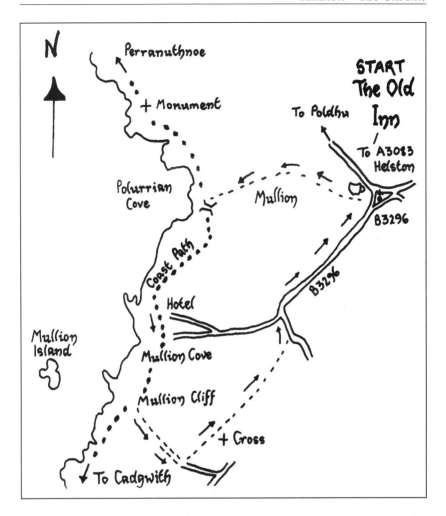

bluebells and campions among them. The views are extensive, reaching across to the site where Marconi sent his first radio signal to Newfoundland, in 1901. On reaching a lookout post keep to the sea side of it and arrive at Mullion Cove Hotel.

Look for the Coast Path sign close to the cannon and take the steep path down into Mullion Cove. You can use the road if you prefer to avoid the steep path. Mullion Island, a prime nesting site for birds, is just offshore. The path descends into the cove via a flight of steps. Turn left here. In a few yards there is a Coast Path sign on your right. Pass behind a house and join the path going over Mullion Cliff. I found it more

55

convenient to keep fairly central going up the hill. The paths wander over this clifftop – take whichever suits you best but you will need to make your way inland here towards a fenced enclosure on your left.

Leave the Coast Path here and take a track on your left, passing a disused slate quarry. The track continues towards a house and gate. After passing through the gate and walking alongside the house you join a road. Look for a footpath sign on your left. There are actually two signs, one pointing from the way you have come and the other to Mullion village. Take this path which is well defined with stone grids or stiles between fields. After crossing into the second field look to your right where you will see a well-preserved Cornish cross. The path continues and soon becomes enclosed. After crossing the last grid of the enclosed path enter a field and keep straight ahead. Ignore the gap on your right and make for a stile and gate ahead. Over the stile, cross the track and enter another enclosed path. Go over the next stile, keeping to the right-hand hedge. Cross over the next stone stile and keep straight on in the next field towards a stile and lane. Turn left. At the next junction turn right and follow the road back into Mullion, about ½ mile. There is a foothpath all the way.

MULLION TO CADGWITH (9½ MILES)

From Mullion Cove the Coast Path continues around Predannack Head. Drop down into Ogo-dour Cove (caves) before climbing again to join the track skirting Vellan Head. The route now goes across moorland, joining the cliffs again at Gew Graze where there is an outcrop of soapstone (French chalk) which was once quarried here. You then reach the chasm of Pigeon Ogo (ogo means cave). This awe inspiring sight affords close ups of nesting seabirds in the breeding season. Continue past Rill Point, along the top of Kynance Cliff when you will drop steeply down into Kynance Cove. The well-walked path continues to Lizard Point, passing old serpentine quarries en route.

The Path continues to follow the coastline, reaching Lizard lighthouse, open to the public at times. Now pass down into Housel Bay. Bass Point is followed by Kilcobben Cove, the site of the Lizard Lifeboat Station. Church Cove, with its delightful thatched cottages, is soon reached, and you join the route of Walk 12. The easily followed path continues close to the cliff edge to pass the Devil's Frying Pan before descending into Cadgwith.

CADGWITH
The Cadgwith Cove Inn

*T*he picturesque cove of Cadgwith is a fitting place to begin this lovely
circuit, which includes a stroll inland through lush farmland, a visit to
the churches of Grade and Landewednack and a walk on a Cornish
hedge. The rugged coastline north of Church Cove, a mecca for artists,
offers spectacular views, with deep chasms being followed by gentle,
flower covered cliffs. You can expect to see tankers and cruise ships on
the horizon while small fishing boats busy themselves around the lobster
pots close to shore.

Two roads approach Cadgwith, both of which plunge down into a cove full of colourwashed, thatched cottages. Full of character and steeped in history, this fishing village maintains a fleet of boats for which the method of launching has remained unchanged for generations. Ten strong men are needed to launch each one and it takes well over an hour to get the whole fleet into the water. On their return, the boats are winched up the beach. Should there be a fierce south-easterly gale then it could be necessary to pull them right up onto the road!

The inn is over 300 years old and remains much as it was in the old smuggling days. Relics of past seafaring adorn the walls of the bar and a log fire burns during the winter months. Summertime sees the lounge bar opened out onto a floodlit patio where drinks and meals can be enjoyed until late in the evening. Singing is a traditional pastime in the cove and visitors and locals join in the rousing choruses which echo round the village.

This Greenalls house serves five real ales and three lagers are on draught, as is Murphy's stout. Local fruit wines are popular and add a further dimension to the more usual wine list. An extensive menu offers a variety of dishes to suit all tastes, with locally caught fish being, of course, particularly popular. A 'specials' board shows the dish of the day and snacks include delicious Cornish pasties and well-filled sandwiches. Children are welcome everywhere except in the main bar area. Their favourite meals are all at one set price.

Opening times are 12 noon to 3 pm and 6 pm to 11 pm or as required, throughout the year. Telephone: 01326 290513.

- **HOW TO GET THERE:** Directions are given from Helston. Take the A3083 Lizard road and in about 8 miles look for a sign on the left for Cadgwith. Follow the road through Ruan Minor and into the cove. The inn is on your right opposite the beach.
- **PARKING:** Parking is difficult in this tightly packed cove. It is best to follow the signs for the public car park which is about 300 yards away. There is a footpath from there back into the cove.
- **LENGTH OF WALK:** 4 miles. Map: OS Landranger 203 Land's End and The Lizard (inn GR 722143).

THE WALK

From the pub turn right for a few yards before reaching a footpath sign for the car park. Follow the path between cottages. On reaching the car park continue to the upper level and make for the road on your left.

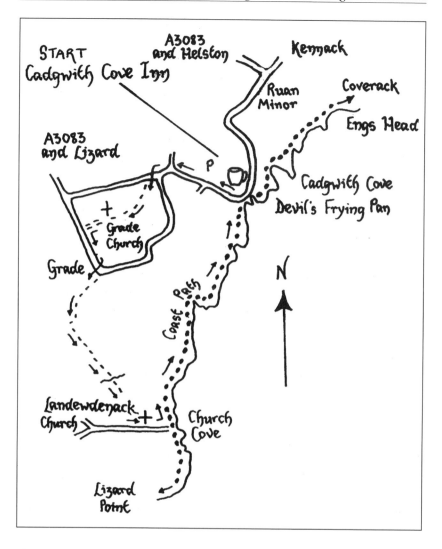

Turn right and walk uphill, ignoring the first left turn. At a road junction turn left, ignore the next left turn, almost immediately, and continue for about 30 yards. Look for a sign in the hedge on your left. Cross the stone stile here and turn right along the hedge, making your way towards the church ahead. Keep slightly left of the church to the next stile. Turn right. Keeping the hedge on your right, continue towards the church. Look for a stone step stile next to a wooden gate and enter the churchyard. This is Grade church. This isolated church stands on the site of an old Norman cruciform building. The present west tower is 14th-century while the bells are dated c1510. Walk left around the church to the exit gate or stile and join a wide, grassy track where you turn left. At the junction with a road turn left.

Continue for about ¼ mile along this road until you see a footpath sign on your right. Follow this and cross a step stile. Keep straight on to the next step stile and continue along the Cornish hedge (these are described in the Perranporth walk) towards a farmhouse ahead. The views here are quite spectacular. You leave the hedge by going down a step stile to join a track. The farm is on your right. Turn left at the track division. Ignore the stile and footpath sign for the Lizard on your right and follow the track as it bends to the left. The track ends in two gates. Cross over the stile on your right where there is a footpath sign. Turn left and keep to the hedge, crossing another stile. Still keeping the hedge on your left, just when the field begins to descend steeply, look for a gap immediately past a rather difficult stile – the waymark is here but it is easier to use the gap. Go straight ahead, skirting the gorse to a track on the right. The track bends to the left. In a few yards look for a narrow path, no sign, on your right. Take this path when you will soon reach a wooden post and stile on your right. Climb the stile and cross the stream. There is no bridge but large stepping stones. Turn left. There is a Countryside Commission sign here. Make for the top of the hill, with a church ahead. You will see a stile and gate in the hedge in front of you. Go over the stile here and onto a track.

You now have the option of either staying on the track, bearing left, to join a lane, or entering the churchyard over a step stile. This is Landewednack, the southernmost parish in England. The church has an interesting lectern made of serpentine rock. On leaving the churchyard, or reaching the lane from the track, turn left. Delightful thatched cottages line the lane all the way down to Church Cove below. This sheltered spot once supported a pilchard industry. The courtyard fish cellars, capstan house, boat store and house are still in situ although converted into modern usage. The route joins the Coast Path just above the cove. It is, however, well worth taking the few extra steps to the boat house. From there turn left between two houses – there is a Cadgwith sign here. Pass through a wooden gate and join the Coast Path.

You are now on National Trust land. Follow the Coast Path sign ahead, keeping to the inland path. Climb a stile then another and emerge onto clifftop fields, with magnificent views. The path along this well-walked section of the Lizard is undulating and very close to the cliff edge in places. It passes small wooden bungalows and offers a wealth of interest to the naturalist.

Just before reaching Cadgwith is the vast crater of Hugga Drigee (Cornish) which is better known as the Devil's Frying Pan. It was probably formed by a cave collapsing. In stormy weather the sea foams in and resembles fat boiling in a pan!

You now enter a courtyard of cottages, National Trust owned, where you cross to an open space by using a step stile. Go over the courtyard, making for the right-hand corner. Take the footpath through the edge of a garden. From here you can look down onto the village, a picture postcard scene. Take the path immediately on your right and continue on the signed path down into Cadgwith.

 ### CADGWITH TO COVERACK (6 MILES)

The Coast Path leaves Cadgwith by turning right just past the inn. From Cadgwith to Enys Head the way is easy to follow and continues along the cliff edge before turning inland at the mouth of the Poltesco valley. In ½ mile you will reach Kennack Sands, a popular place for caravanners. Leave Kennack by keeping to the seaward path where the route is easily followed. Cut across the headland of Carrick Luz. A stiff climb takes you up to Beagles Point. As the Coast Path approaches Coverack you will need to turn inland to Chynhalls but can rejoin it to take a route around Chynalls Point if you wish. From here it is a comfortable walk down to Coverack where you enter the village by the Paris Hotel.

COVERACK
The Paris Hotel
❧

A gentle coastal walk followed by a stretch on the road. Field paths complete the circuit, which is distinguished by the variety of terrain and scenery. There is a good midway 'stop-off' at Roskilly's Farm where you can partake of home-made ice cream or maybe a cream tea. A group of well-preserved gypsy caravans are a great attraction here. There is just one steep hill climb and the route is suitable for most age groups. Leave time to explore the delightful village and beach.

Coverack's pretty cove attracts many visitors. Fishing continues as an industry but windsurfing is also taught here and children play happily in the rock pools left by a receding tide. Thatched cottages cluster along the sea front and attractive shops sell a variety of local crafts. The beach is a mecca for geologists. It is here that they come to see the junction between the earth's mantle and the oceanic crust, known as the 'Moho'.

The complex geology of the Lizard is responsible for the spectacular and colourful cliffs which make up this scenic area.

It is rather surprising to find a pub known as the Paris Hotel in this location – one might expect it to bear a more local name. It does, however, recall an incident which occurred here in 1899 when an express liner with twin screws was stranded for three weeks on a reef known as the Manacles, east of Dean Point. Known as *The City of Paris*, she was eventually refloated and entered service again in 1901, being then renamed *The Philadelphia*. She was scrapped in 1923 but her name continues.

The Paris Hotel was built in 1907 by the St Austell Brewery. It is now a Greenalls house serving well-kept Boddingtons and Bass along with Newquay Steam and Flowers Bitter. Caffrey's Irish ale and Guinness are also available, and a comprehensive wine list. The comfortable restaurant, for which there is a supper licence, has wide windows giving a scenic coastal outlook. During the summer the garden is well used. Overlooking the sea, the old lifeboat house and a stretch of spectacular coastline, one can happily make a drink and snack last for some time! Fish is, of course, a feature of the menu and the landlord, a keen fisherman himself, helps to maintain supplies. Crab and large prawns are served with salads and a brown malted-wheat roll. Swordfish steak or fresh pollock are other favourites. Good sirloin, rump or fillet steaks are offered in the restaurant or perhaps a duck breast coated with a honey sauce may be your choice. Vegetarians are not forgotten, with home-made dishes which include nut rissoles or tagliatelle in a white sauce. The bar menu always includes a home-made soup. A Paris Cliffhanger – white crusty French roll or brown malted wheat filled with salad garnish and choice of cheese, meat, fish or chicken – is delicious. A jacket potato or a leek and mushroom quiche may tempt you too. The varied desserts are not for the calorie counter! Children are welcome away from the bar.

Opening times: 11 am to 3 pm and 6 pm to 11 pm in the summer, 12 noon to 3 pm and 7 pm to 11 pm in the winter. The restaurant extends these hours. Telephone: 01326 280258.

• **HOW TO GET THERE:** From the A3083 between Helston and the Lizard take the B3293 just south of RNAS Culdrose. Follow the signs for Coverack at the next roundabout. Continue on this road until you reach a crossroads with St Keverne to the left and Coverack to the right. The pub is at the end of the village.

• **PARKING:** There is very limited parking at the pub but you will find a car park beyond it on the headland which has an honesty box. There is also a large public car park as you enter the village.

• **LENGTH OF WALK:** 5 miles. Map: OS Landranger 204 Truro, Falmouth and surrounding area (inn GR 785182).

THE WALK

From the Paris Hotel walk along the sea front until the road bears to the left. Keep straight on here, following a tarmac drive. There is a wooden Coast Path sign. The drive passes between houses and narrows to a path. Just before a gate turn right, signed. You are making for Lowland Point which is well named as it reaches out to sea from beach level. Follow the path over a stile and a wooden bridge. The route is well defined and easy to follow. As you approach the Point there are various paths but keep seawards at beach level. You will soon be able to see the scar of Dean Quarry ahead. The quarrying gear and pier block the coastal path but it is well signed around the area. Leave the Coast Path here.

Our route now skirts the quarry by taking the path to the left. This wends its way uphill quite steeply. You will probably be surprised to find a picnic table and benches when you reach the summit! You now join an enclosed path. As you reach the end of the path and a gate turn left at a footpath sign. You will soon join a track. Turn right here, following the St Keverne sign not the Coverack one which goes off to the left. Keep on this track until it joins a road where you will turn left.

Continue on this road for about ½ mile until you reach a junction. Turn left to arrive at Roskilly's Farm where they produce ice cream and other dairy products. Pause for a rest and refreshment perhaps? The route now follows the road for about ¼ mile to where you will see a sign on the left to Trebarveth Farm. Immediately adjacent to this drive is a stile and footpath sign for Coverack. Follow the well-defined path across fields. You will see large boulders of exposed rock here. Join a track which leads to Trevalsoe Farm and buildings. Turn left and continue down the track for about 100 yards. Look for a stile on the left, waymarked. Pass a cattle enclosure, ignore all gaps and make for an enclosed path. You will soon reach Boscarnon, a group of cottages and a house. Walk about 50 yards along the drive, past the last house on the left, and look for a footpath sign in the hedge. Take the path here, bearing to the left and then to the right through a gap. You now join another enclosed path through a wooded area. On reaching a cross-path

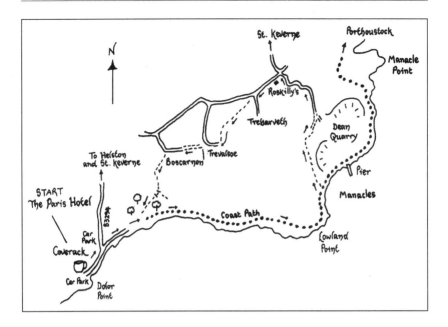

with a stile either side of it keep straight on over the stiles. You will soon rejoin the Coast Path along the driveway to the houses where you began the walk. Continue back through the village to the pub.

COVERACK TO MAWNAN CHURCH (20 MILES)

The Coast Path from Coverack to Mawnan Smith presents some problems. The map shows it passing through Dean Quarry but you may well encounter some diversions here. At Godrevy Cove, approximately 1 mile from Dean Point, the route makes its way inland before turning seawards again to reach Porthoustock. From there it continues inland until reaching the village of Porthallow. It then maintains a cliff edge path as far as Gillan Creek. There is no ferry here and it is necessary to go inland. Leave the Coast Path via a signed footpath before reaching the creek. Continue on the path at Flushing and join a road. Turn right and make for Carne at the head of the creek where there is a bridge. Turn right along the creek. Pass through St Anthony and rejoin the Coast Path round Denis Head. It is now a lovely walk along the estuary of the Helford River where at Helford there should be a ferry to cross to Helford Passage. The path continues to Durgan where we join the route of Walk 14 as far as Mawnan church.

MAWNAN SMITH
The Red Lion
❧❀❧

*A lovely walk, suitable for all age groups, incorporating splendid
coastal scenery with field paths and quiet lanes. A short detour to the
charming estuary-side hamlet of Durgan is also possible. Paths are
waymarked and are all easily followed.*

Mawnan Smith is a large village closely associated with the National
Trust holdings of Bosloe, Mawnan and Glendurgan Garden, the latter
containing many rare and exotic plants which thrive in this sheltered
part of Cornwall. There are many walks linking National Trust and
coastal paths, all of which include splendid views across the estuary of
the Helford river.

The attractive, thatched Red Lion inn dates back to the 15th century.
Originally a row of five cottages, it is known to have been a pub for over
100 years. A sympathetic modernisation has enhanced the original

architecture with a choice of comfortable bars, a dining room and a children's room. Amid low beams and old wood, the friendly staff give a warm welcome.

The menu offers a variety of dishes. Starters, grills, seafood, vegetarian meals and puddings are included. One very unusual starter is a combination of peppers, king prawns, garlic mushrooms, salsa, garlic and herb dips! A mixed grill for the really hungry needs a large plate to hold the lamb cutlet, steak, gammon, sausage, kidneys and fried egg. Chicken in lobster sauce is another mouthwatering favourite. For the vegetarian there is bean, celery and coriander chilli or a mushroom stroganoff. A Greenhalls house, well-kept ales including Bass, Worthington and a guest beer are served. Keg Heineken, Steam Pils and Stella Artois are the lagers offered here. There is a comprehensive wine list.

Opening times are 11 am to 3 pm and 6 pm to 11 pm throughout the year. Sunday 12 noon to 3 pm and 6.30 pm to 10.30 pm. Telephone: 01326 250026.

> • **HOW TO GET THERE:** Directions are given from Truro. Leave Truro via the bypass taking the A39 to Falmouth. Cross the junction with the A393 from Redruth. Continue on the A39, negotiate two roundabouts and take the first sign for Mabe (Burnthouse). From Mabe the road is well signed to Mawnan Smith crossing between College and Argal reservoirs.
>
> • **PARKING:** At the pub.
>
> • **LENGTH OF WALK:** 3 miles or 3½ miles if you decide to visit Durgan. Map: OS Landranger 204 Truro, Falmouth and surrounding area (inn GR 780286).

THE WALK

From the pub car park turn left and walk up the road for just under ½ mile until you see a footpath sign on your left. Go over the stile here and walk diagonally right towards another stile, onto a lane. This cuts a corner and avoids some road walking. Turn left at the lane and join a footpath on your right leading to a National Trust car park. Go through the car park, following signs. Our route goes left on reaching the lane again at the point where you will see a stile, an acorn sign and a National Trust plaque, 'Bosloe'. However, I would suggest that you turn right here and walk down into the village of Durgan, a remote hamlet whose shoreline shows evidence of high tides as the Helford river joins the sea. There are a handful of cottages and a village school, dated 1876, now a residence, almost on the beach. After exploring, walk back up the hill and rejoin the Coast Path route.

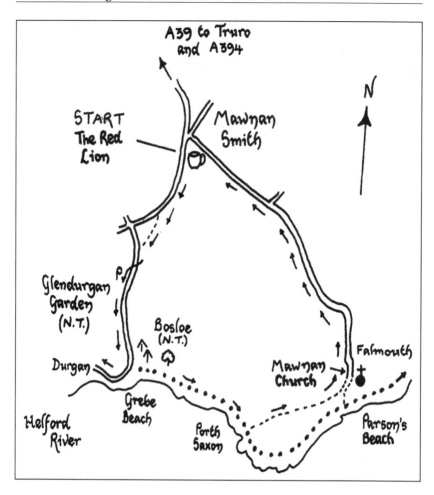

Follow the path adjacent to woodland and continue across the field. Bosloe House is on your left. Its position, overlooking the entrance to the Helford river, makes this handsome residence, split into three portions, the flagship of the Trust's Cornwall holiday holdings. Grebe Beach lies below. Continue to follow the path, clearly marked and much used, enjoying the scenery of the sheltered southern section of the Coast Path.

The route now continues above Porth Saxon when you will arrive at a junction of paths. Our route follows the Coast Path above the cliffs until you reach a wide gap into an open field. Walk across to a stile leading into a wood with a National Trust sign, 'Mawnan Glebe'. You will soon arrive at an acorn sign with an arrow pointing straight ahead.

Do not follow this direction but bear left towards a flight of wooden steps. Go up these and join a path, passing over two stiles to reach Mawnan church. Unfortunately, the church is not open at all times. You will now lane walk back to Mawnan Smith, about 1 mile. The lane carries little traffic and is extremely pleasant.

 ### MAWNAN TO PORTLOE (24 MILES, EXCLUDING DIVERSIONS)

The path from below Mawnan church continues near the cliff edge down towards Falmouth. Continue through Maen Porth to Swanpool Beach when you will be in the outskirts of Falmouth. Pendennis Castle stands on the promontory of Pendennis Point. A ferry operates from the quay across to St Mawes where there is another artillery castle. There is now a problem. To cross to Place means crossing the Percuil river. Unfortunately, in 1996, there is no ferry available. The nearest crossing is by road bridge some 2½ miles along the A3078 at Trethem Mill. There is a footpath from here which joins a minor road leading to Portscatho, where you can rejoin the Coast Path. The total journey is 3¾ miles. It also means that you will have missed the Coast Path from St Mawes around Zone Point. To include this would mean a round trip of 13¾ miles (see OS Landranger sheet 204 Truro, Falmouth and surrounding area).

The 4 miles from Portscatho to Nare Head offer no complications apart from a climb up to the headland. From Nare Head to where we join the route of Walk 15 on Rosen Cliff is fine cliff walking, much of it on National Trust ground.

PORTLOE
The Ship Inn

This lovely part of south Cornwall offers the walker a wealth of flora along a spectacular coastline. A few minor climbs and one steep downhill section make this ever changing route one to be savoured and suitable for most age groups. An opportunity to seek crustaceans and seaweeds as you cross close to a rocky shore adds an extra dimension to the walk.

Portloe is an attractive, small fishing village. Boats are drawn up on the shore where cottages, a pub and a teashop cluster together. This must be one of Cornwall's most unspoilt villages. Tucked in among steep cliffs it is served by narrow lanes which do not encourage heavier vehicles. The colourwashed cottages glow with red valerian and bright hanging baskets bring another splash of colour throughout the summer.

The Ship Inn was rebuilt in 1908 after a fire. Painted a picturesque blue and white with traditional roses around the doors and windows, it offers a warm welcome throughout the year. Its cosy bar is comfortably furnished with an open fire for those colder days. Good home-cooked food is offered, the menu for which is displayed on a board and changes frequently. Specialities are the home-made bread rolls which accompany almost everything. As one would expect, fish occupies a prominent place on the menu with crab or prawn sandwiches being ever popular. As an alternative, a generous ploughman's with mackerel or ham, a substantial soup or something with chips might be your choice. Cream teas are served during the afternoon, while tea and coffee are always available. Packed lunches are provided too. A St Austell Brewery house, Trelawney Pride and St Austell Best are the popular real ales on offer here. XXXX Mild and various lagers and Guinness are also on draught. Wines are sold by glass or bottle. Children are welcome and will find facilities for their use and a menu of their own.

Opening times are Easter to October open all day. Winter months 11.30 am to 3 pm and 6.30 pm to 11 pm. Telephone: 01872 501356.

- **HOW TO GET THERE:** From the A390 St Austell-Truro road make your way to Tregony. If approaching from St Austell, your choice should be the B3287, signed 'Tregony' and 'St Mawes', just past Hewas Water. From Tregony take the St Mawes road, the A3078. In about 2 miles look for a sign to Portloe on your left. You will need to go through the village and up the hill, where you will find the pub on your right.
- **PARKING:** There is parking just past the pub.
- **LENGTH OF WALK:** 4½ miles. Map: OS Landranger 204 Truro, Falmouth and surrounding area (inn GR 938396).

THE WALK

From the pub turn right and walk uphill for about 200 yards to a group of houses known as Sunny Corner. As you continue up the lane look for steps in the hedge leading to a metal framed stile. Go over this and you will see another stile ahead. Make your way diagonally across the next field towards the top right-hand corner where you will climb another stile and reach a lane. You are now in the village of Camels. Walk between the houses and continue along the lane to a crossroads. Turn left. In about ¼ mile you will reach a fork. Take the left-hand lane, which is very narrow, and continue for about ½ mile to a car park on your right. There is a viewing point just above the car park where you can enjoy the views across Nare Head. This prominent headland is owned by the National Trust together with much of the surrounding land.

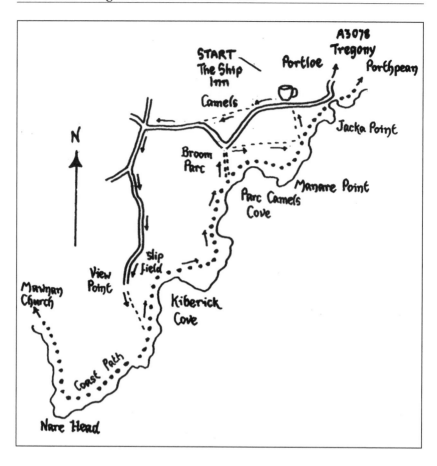

Opposite the car park you will see a gate and stile on your left. Over
the stile you will be looking down a steep valley towards the sea. Keep
to the left of the valley, walking diagonally towards the fence. Look for
a stile adjacent to a National Trust signboard. Go over the stile to join the
Coast Path.

You are now on Rosen Cliff. You will be able to enjoy some truly
South Cornwall scenery while pursuing the undulating path along
this section of the coastline. Above Kiberick Cove, popular with anglers,
is a slip field, a flat area which has at some time dropped about 20 feet.
Some say it happened in the 19th century while others date it much
earlier. Beyond the Blouth the Coast Path drops almost to beach level at
Parc Camels Cove. Pause a few minutes here and explore the seashore
for a variety of crustaceans and seaweeds. The path now climbs steeply

towards a solitary white house known as Broom Parc. Owned by the Trust, it stands close by a group of Monterey pines. The Coast Path now rounds Manare Point to the Watch Rock before descending the Jacka into Portloe.

However, the route we take leaves the Coast Path at Broom Parc house and makes slightly inland over field paths before reaching the village. Take a left-hand path below the house which will bring you up to a small car park and the house entrance. Turn right through a field gate. Go through another gate. At the next one leave the track and bear left across open clifftop towards a wood. This sheltered woodland is very pleasant on a hot day. The path is somewhat steep as it descends to the village. Take a left fork and then another which passes beside the Tregain Tea Rooms. Turn left at the lane and walk uphill back to the pub.

 PORTLOE TO CHARLESTOWN (15 MILES)

From Portloe the path climbs up some steep steps onto the cliffs at Portloe Point. The path is narrow in places en route to Portholland, which is the next village on the south coast route. At Porthluney Cove you will need to leave the cliffs and turn inland at right angles, then cross a field and join a road which you follow for 300 yards to the beach. Keep on the road for a few yards before rejoining the path on the other side. Cross a stile beside the road and take a track leading across a field parallel to the cliff edge. Keep to the seaward side at the boundary of the next field. Dodman Point will be your next headland, National Trust territory.

From the Dodman to Mevagissey, which is 4¾ miles, there is a well-walked path with good views. Mevagissey with its narrow streets, variety of shops and colourful fishing boats is a place to explore. On then to Pentewan. Cross the river by the road bridge here and follow the Coast Path signs to rejoin the path past Gamas Point. The next headland is Black Head. You will need to leave the coast here and walk inland to Trenarren. Road walk from here to a gate a few yards west of Castle Gotha Farm, which is signed. The field path back to the coast is quite clear to where you rejoin the Coast Path above Porthpean. Easy walking now on a well-made path to the village of Charlestown.

CHARLESTOWN
The Rashleigh Arms
❦

This walk, which starts at the tiny port of Charlestown, the scene of china clay exports for decades, incorporates clifftops with springy turf and a pleasant path over golf links, past beautiful houses and gardens – all just to the south of busy St Austell. A short detour en route will take you down into Carlyon Bay with its popular leisure complex.

Charles Rashleigh gave his name to this village, developing the port in the late 18th century. Steeped in a historical saga of mineral wealth the Rashleigh family's colourful story reflects the ups and downs of the precarious mining ventures that have dogged Cornwall's past and present. Changing times have seen a move away from the china clay industry here and while the shutes are still in situ the harbour is given over to tall sailing ships, recalling the days when these magnificent vessels were to be seen all around our coasts. Charlestown has hosted

TV crews making such well-known series as *The Onedin Line* and *Darwin*. *The Eagle has Landed* was filmed here some years ago.

Our pub, the Rashleigh Arms, was built originally to store china clay. Now a freehouse with a spacious restaurant and bar, it offers a varied menu. The pasties here are delicious and the fish meals, particularly local crab, are ever popular while the chef prides himself on a good mix of traditional, vegetarian and local dishes. A selection of eight real ales should provide sufficient choice for everyone. These are complemented by Murphy's stout, Worthington or Guinness on draught, the usual lagers and ciders in the bar and a good selection of wines in the restaurant. A large, sheltered garden is an ideal place to eat and drink on a fine day. Children have a room of their own and a special menu.

Opening times: 11 am to 11 pm on Monday to Saturday throughout the year. Sundays 12 noon to 10.30 pm. Telephone: 01726 73635.

- **HOW TO GET THERE:** Leave the A390 St Austell-Liskeard road at its junction with the A3061, signed 'Charlestown'. This goes straight into Charlestown, where you will see the pub on your left.
- **PARKING:** Adjacent to the pub. There is also a large public car park opposite.
- **LENGTH OF WALK:** 5 miles. Map OS Landranger 204 Truro, Falmouth and surrounding area (inn GR 038516).

THE WALK

From the pub walk down towards the harbour. At the roundabout keep to the left. You will now be able to look down onto the tall ships below. As you reach the sea turn left through a gap alongside a chained drive where you will meet the Coast Path.

Walk uphill to a gate, go through this and enter a wood. Keep straight on, ignoring gaps, to the top of the hill. Turn right through a gate and continue to another gate, keeping the hedge on your left. You will now meet a road with the Porth Avalon Hotel opposite. Turn right along the footpath and then right again onto another path, waymarked. Continue along an enclosed path in front of some houses. Flowering shrubs and bushes make this a pleasant path to walk. You will reach a gate leading to an open, grassed area with Carlyon Bay Hotel ahead. Follow the hotel boundary fence and pass through another gate beside a large car park. You are now above Carlyon Bay. If you wish to detour to the beach and leisure complex then do so when the path joins the road just ahead from here. Our route crosses the road and follows the

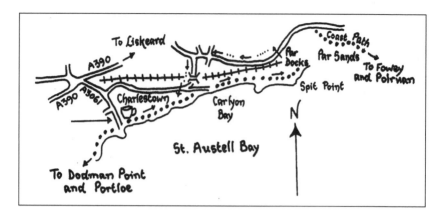

signed Coast Path straight ahead. Keep right, along the path, as you approach the golf course. Continue to follow the well-marked route, keeping close to the cliffs as you progress across the course.

You will soon see the chimneys of Par Docks. Not a particularly pretty sight but a necessary one for this part of the county. It is very pleasant walking here as the path wends its way round towards Spit Beach. You will see a line of trees leading up from the beach. There is a path here which takes you inland away from the Coast Path.

Turn left along this enclosed path with dockyard buildings around you. On reaching a car park and the road turn left. You now have approximately one mile of road walking. There is a wide grass verge and some path. It is, however, a busy road so care is needed. Continue past a garden centre where refreshments can be obtained if required. Cross over an entrance to an industrial estate before reaching a turning on the left. Turn here towards the golf course which you can see ahead and walk up this wide drive, busy at times. Go under the railway bridge and onto the top of the hill to a four-way junction. Turn left towards Carlyon Bay and rejoin the Coast Path above the beach.

You will now have a pleasant stroll, downhill, retracing your steps into Charlestown.

 ### CHARLESTOWN TO POLRUAN (8 MILES)

Follow the pub walk route from Charlestown harbour as far as Spit Beach. You will need to follow the path inland from the beach alongside the fence which is the boundary of the china clay works. Turn right, east, along the road, under two bridges. Continue to follow the road

The harbour at Charlestown now frequented by tall sailing ships

through Par, turning right at junctions, taking signs for Par Sands, about 1¼ miles. From the sands the Coast Path runs between cliff edge and pastures to Polkerris where you will find refreshments and an inn on the beach. Notice the old lime kilns here. The Path continues from just above the harbour and climbs steeply through a wood. You will emerge onto open grassland as you walk the 2 miles to Gribbin Head, National Trust. A red and white daymark dominates the headland. The route now descends to Polridmouth where a stream runs down into the cove from a lake above, a lovely place. A clearly defined path now leads you over cliffs and fields to Fowey, which you will enter close to St Catherine's Castle. You will descend to Readymoney Cove before following the road into Fowey. As you enter the town look for a sign on your right for the passenger ferry to Polruan. This operates every 15 minutes throughout the day and will take you across to continue the journey from Polruan.

POLRUAN
The Lugger

❧✿❧

*This walk takes you through National Trust ground with well-kept paths
and stiles. A steep climb over a headland above Lantic Bay offers
splendid views of this lovely part of the south coast, then the inland route
follows a path through woodland and pasture above Pont Pill, a creek of
the Fowey river. Kenneth Grahame's* Wind in the Willows *comes to mind
as you walk along here. This well-marked circuit is one I never tire of.
The sight and sound of water accompanies you almost all the way.*

Polruan and Fowey face each other across the estuary of the river
Fowey. A bustling, deep water harbour, it is capable of offering an
anchorage to cruise ships as well as to those associated with the china
clay industry. Polruan's steep village street leads down to the quay and
the foot passenger ferry while boat builders are busily engaged in plying
their craft in the sheds close by.

The Lugger is as near to the water as it can be. Known to be an inn for 300 years, its present day bar was once a sail loft. Some of its business comes from the water traffic passing close to its door while land-based locals and holidaymakers enjoy the views up river. Wood and brass play a large part in the pub's decoration, nautical pictures decorate the walls and a cheerful fire gives comfort on a blustery evening. The dining room, where children are welcome, is spacious and comfortable. It is hardly surprising to find fish occupying a major place on the menu – and it is certainly not everywhere that can claim that fish caught today is eaten today. Lamb and beef, pork and chicken feature too, while vegetarians should be well satisfied with the dishes offered for them. Bar snacks and light meals are advertised on a 'specials' board which changes frequently. Real ale drinkers will be spoilt for choice with brews that include Hicks Special, Bosun's and Tinners Bitter, Trelawney Pride and XXXX. Lagers on draught and bottled along with Guinness and good house wines are also available.

Opening times: 11 am to 11 pm every day throughout the year. Food is served from 12 noon to 2 pm and 7 pm to 9 pm in the summer. Winter food times are 12.30 pm to 2 pm and 7 pm to 8.30 pm.

Telephone: 01726 870007.

- **HOW TO GET THERE:** Directions are given from the A390 St Austell-Liskeard road. *For the route via the car ferry from Fowey*, look for a 'Fowey' sign at St Blazey, 2 miles from St Austell, leading you onto the A3082. At a junction with the B3269 take the sign for the car ferry, 'Bodinnick'. Ferries run continuously during the day. From Bodinnick follow signs for Polruan. Drive down the village to the quay for the pub (see parking notes). *For the route without using the car ferry*, from the small town of Lostwithiel look for a sign for Lerryn. Turn right along this lane and continue through St Veep and Penpoll and on to Lanteglos Highway. Follow the signs for Polruan, not Bodinnick, when you reach this point. NB: There are some very narrow lanes on this route.

- **PARKING:** Very limited parking is available on the quay, for which there is a charge. There is a car park at the top of the hill just before embarking on the steep hill through the village. It is signed and is the most convenient place to park though again one has to pay.

- **LENGTH OF WALK:** 4 miles. Maps: the walk begins on OS Landranger 200 Newquay and Bodmin or on 204 Truro, Falmouth and surrounding area. It then continues on 201 Plymouth and Launceston (inn GR 127510).

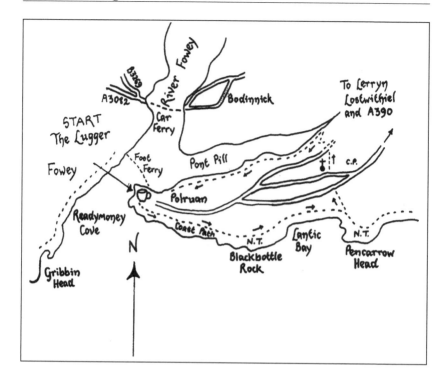

THE WALK

From the pub turn right up the steep flight of steps facing you. On reaching the lane above turn right and continue between the tightly packed cottages until reaching Battery Lane. You can make a slight detour here by keeping straight ahead to reach an old watch house guarding the entrance to Fowey harbour. Turn up Battery Lane, which rises steeply, until you reach a track leading straight ahead which you will take. Follow the footpath sign towards a car park where you will also see a coastguard station. Keeping the car park on your left, you will soon join a road. Keep straight ahead for about 100 yards where you will see a Coast Path sign on your right, signed for Lantic Bay, Pencarrow Head and Lantivet Bay. Take this path and pass through the gate onto National Trust land.

Join the South Cornwall Coast Path here. The most superb panoramas now greet you as you look across towards the entrance to Fowey harbour and the coastline beyond. In about ¾ mile Lantic Bay will come into view, a lovely sandy beach, quite isolated. There is a steep path down to it with access about ¼ mile ahead. You will now see a

National Trust sign indicating that you are at Blackbottle Rock. Keep right here and descend some steps before ascending a very steep section of coastal path above Lantic Bay. Continue to the top of the hill where there is a junction of paths. Climb the stile and turn immediately left through a gate. This is where you leave the Coast Path and turn inland.

Keeping the hedge on your right, continue along a well-defined path to a gate and stile leading onto a road. Cross over and turn right. At the sign for Pont and Lanteglos church turn left. There is a National Trust car park here. Walk down the lane to reach the church and enter the churchyard by the first gate. Walk straight ahead until you come to a white gate. Go through this and then another towards some cottages. This is an idyllic spot. Almost opposite across the lane to your left are some steps leading into a wood, signed 'Pont Mill' and 'Hall Walk'. Go down these to where, almost immediately on your left, there are more steps. Ascend these, signed 'Footpath to Polruan'. Climb a stile into a field where you follow the path uphill to be greeted with a superb view of Pont Pill, a creek of the river Fowey. In the spring primroses will carpet the path. The next mile of this undulating walk is one of the most beautiful I have ever trodden.

At a fork keep left and at a cross-track turn right for a couple of yards, then left. You are now walking through a lightly wooded area with convenient benches along the route as you approach Polruan. At a junction of paths turn right down some steps then turn left and so back to the harbour and the pub.

 POLRUAN TO POLPERRO (6 MILES)

Follow the pub walk route as far as Lantic Bay. The next section of the South Coast Path to Polperro is partially managed by the National Trust with its usual well-marked paths. There are, however, some parts in between where the way may not be so easily defined. Coast Path signs are at relevant points. From Lantic Bay the next headland is Pencarrow Head. On then to Lantivet Bay with some sandy coves and sloping cliffs behind. There was once a quay here. Climb then to Lansallos Head, around 450 feet high. Descend to sea level at East Coombe and from there continue onto National Trust land again at Chapel Cliff. The walk from here into Polperro is on good footpaths, with splendid views of the village.

WALK 18

POLPERRO
The Crumplehorn Inn
❧

To walk along the cliffs from Polperro to Talland is an experience not to be missed. Much of the area is National Trust owned, part of the 38 acres donated by the authoress Miss Angela Brazil in 1948, and is maintained to their usual high standard. Delightful Talland Bay is just the place to relax and perhaps enjoy an ice cream or cup of tea before returning to Polperro, up the only steep hill of the route.

The picture postcard Cornish village of Polperro, a mecca for artists and photographers, is not designed for traffic! A wide stream beside the main street rushes down to meet the sea while pedestrians take things more slowly and enjoy the jumble of cottages, shops and inns as they stroll down to the harbour, tucked in between Peak Rock and Downed Point.

It is difficult to decide which of the dishes described in the extensive menu at the Crumplehorn are the most popular. The owner is also the chef whose imaginative meals include fresh fish caught by Polperro's fishing fleet. That king of fish the sea bass or a whole sole on the bone are just two of the possibilities. A fresh seafood platter is a magnificent collage of local fish, its different textures, colours and cooking being such that you would be advised to have a camera at the ready. Meat and poultry are by no means forgotten – champagne chicken, steak and scallop pie or roast duck with black cherry sauce are examples. The more usual bar snacks include home-made soup or crab cocktail and ploughman's, fisherman's or cattleman's lunches, all served with salad and crusty roll. Puddings come with Cornish clotted cream or ice cream while a children's menu offers the usual favourites. A note on the menu states that 'we do not serve fast food. We serve good food as fast as we can'! An added attraction is the outstanding Cornish ales served here. Instead of the beer being 'fined' or cleared of impurities at the brewery, this is done after delivery to the pub. The settling process is thus simplified and the beer has its own special taste. The Crumplehorn is the only inn in Cornwall to do this. The brews include St Austell HSD and XXXX Mild. Draught Bass and scrumpy along with a guest ale which is changed weekly are among the other beers. Lagers and a comprehensive wine list are also offered.

Opening times are 11 am to 11 pm throughout the year. Sunday 12 noon to 3 pm and 7 pm to 10.30 pm, open in the afternoon during the summer. Telephone: 01503 272348.

- **HOW TO GET THERE:** Directions are given from the A38 Bodmin to Plymouth road. About 1 mile east of Liskeard look for a sign for Looe off the dual carriageway. Turn onto the B3252 and continue to follow the Looe signs. After passing through that town Polperro is signed via the A387. Approaching the village by a steep hill you will see the inn on your left with its large mill wheel turning beside it.
- **PARKING:** Use the large public car park immediately opposite the pub. There is no access for traffic down the village street – goods vehicles and residents' cars are the only permitted vehicles.
- **LENGTH OF WALK:** 3 miles. Map: OS Landranger 201 Plymouth and Launceston (inn GR 205516).

THE WALK

From the inn turn left and walk beside the stream towards the harbour. Continue to follow harbour signs when you reach a fork. Bear right here where there is also a Coast Path sign, rather obscure and low down on the wall.

 Keep to the left of the harbour, walking between some cottages, and join a tarmac path. The route now takes you uphill with views across the harbour to Peak Rock – an excellent place to take photographs. The path is easily followed and much walked. You will soon be on National Trust land known as The Warren.

You will reach a sign marking 1 mile from Polperro where the path splits. Keep to the lower one for Talland and Looe. In about ½ mile you will reach a joint war memorial for Polperro and Looe set on Downend Point, a fitting place to remember men who probably spent much of their lives at sea.

Continue along the well-maintained path towards Talland Bay, which will come into view as you round the headland, a small beach surrounded by cliffs ablaze with bright yellow gorse in the spring. A new path has been constructed here which takes you away from the cliff edge. The Coast Path meets with a tarmac path which leads down to the beach. If you are in need of refreshment now is your chance to take advantage of a popular licensed cafe about 200 yards past the beach on the Looe side. This convenient stop is open from Easter until the end of October and is known as The Smugglers Rest.

However, to continue the walk there is no need to actually go down to the beach but turn left at the path which soon becomes a steep lane. Near to the summit is a welcome bench and just past it a footpath sign on the left. You can choose to take this path which leads back to the Coast Path and retrace your steps to Polperro. Our route continues along the lane. Pass the first right-hand junction and walk towards a small housing estate and a school. At the T-junction turn left and walk down a steep, narrow road, known as Talland Hill. There is a traffic restriction sign at the top so you can walk almost undisturbed to Polperro below.

No doubt you will wish to spend some time exploring this delightful village. Much photograped and painted, it has many byways to distract you. Choose your own route back to the Crumplehorn Inn.

POLPERRO TO KINGSAND (21½ MILES)

Follow the pub walk from Polperro harbour to Talland Bay. The Coast Path from Talland to Whitesand Bay has very varied terrain. The first 4 miles to Looe are easily walked with splendid scenery. Cross the river

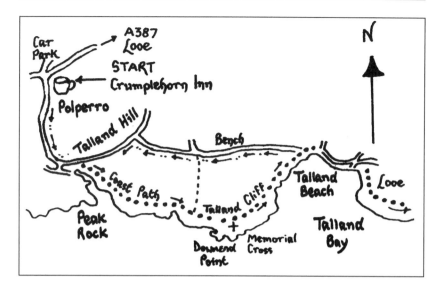

from West to East Looe either by ferry or the road bridge and rejoin the Coast Path along the east cliffs from a lane opposite the Guildhall. The island ½ mile offshore is known as Looe or St George's Island.

Pass through Millandreath where a sandy beach is surrounded by a holiday complex. The route now leads up through trees to Bodigga Cliff, National Trust land. In about 1½ miles, following signs, you arrive at Seaton. From here you can beach walk at low tide to Downderry where you pick up the Coast Path again to Portwrinkle. You will need to turn inland after about 1 mile, signed. The sandy expanse of Whitesand Bay now comes into view. It is possible to beach walk - possible, but risky. Not only do you have dangerous currents but you have a Ministry of Defence firing range on Tregantle Cliff, 1 mile along the route. Warnings are given by the hoisting of red flags. The road walk has a path running close beside it most of the way and Rame Head beckons you on. By the time you reach the junction where the next walk joins the Coast Path it is wide with soft grass and wildflowers. The walk across Rame Head and Penlee Point is a delight. You enter Cawsand where the road is also the Coast Path and walk onto the twin village of Kingsand.

Refreshments along this long section can be obtained at Looe, Millandreath, Seaton, Downderry, Portwrinkle and, seasonally, above Whitesand Bay.

KINGSAND
The Halfway House
❦

There are many approaches to the chapel-topped headland of Rame. I have chosen a field path start to this walk which culminates in spectacular coastal scenery as you approach the long distance path. A variety of field and sea birds with wildflowers in abundance can be enjoyed – I am not sure who was the most startled as I came across two young deer who danced along in front of me for several hundred yards. Wide grassy paths and steps up slopes make this route suitable for most age groups.

Sometimes called 'the forgotten corner of Cornwall', the Coast Path here offers some of its most spectacular scenery across the sheltered shoreline of Cawsand Bay. The Halfway House marks the point at which the twin villages of Kingsand and Cawsand meet. These days the river Tamar forms the boundary between Devon and Cornwall but until 1835

Kingsand was in Devon and Cawsand in Cornwall. The boundary cross can be seen in the wall opposite the inn. This pink-washed pub tucked in at the bottom of the steep village street is just a few yards from the sea front. Houses cluster round while a few village shops provide a variety of goods.

The Halfway House is a friendly, welcoming place where locals and visitors chat happily together. The busy tourist season winds down to a more relaxed atmosphere at other times of the year when a glowing wood-burning stove offers comfort on a chilly day. A comfortably furnished bar and restaurant are enhanced with copper covered tables and local sea and landscapes. Flowers are a feature both inside and out, hanging baskets blooming in profusion during the summer. The chef prides himself on a varied menu with fish dishes reflecting the enviable position of this old inn. The restaurant caters for the more serious diner while a good selection of daily 'specials' are available in the bar. With dishes such as cassoulet of brill or delicious crab puffs, ragout of turbot or monkfish with peppers one may be forgiven for not looking any further along the menu. However, a chicken basque or lamb noisettes could be your preference. Delicious sweets and puddings tempt the most committed weightwatcher. The walker will, no doubt, be in need of liquid refreshment. Here you will find Bass, Charrington and Worthington ales along with Flowers Original and a guest beer. A good wine list is available too. Children are not allowed in the bars but are made welcome in the restaurant.

Opening times: 11 am to 3 pm and 6 pm to 11 pm, 12 noon to 3 pm and 7 pm to 11 pm on Sunday. Telephone: 01752 822279.

> • **HOW TO GET THERE:** Kingsand lies in Cawsand Bay south of Torpoint, to which a car ferry operates from Plymouth. Leave Torpoint by the A374 for Antony and join the B3274 for Millbrook. From Millbrook take the unclassified road, signed 'Kingsand'. On reaching the village follow the width restriction signs down the village street. The pub is at the bottom on the right. A foot ferry operates during the summer months between Cawsand and Plymouth.
>
> • **PARKING:** A public car park is immediately adjacent to the pub.
>
> • **LENGTH OF WALK:** 5½ miles. Map: OS Landranger 201 Plymouth and Launceston (inn GR 435503).

THE WALK

From the pub turn right into Garrett Street which joins Kingsand and

Cawsand. As you approach the Smugglers Inn turn right into St Andrews and walk between houses as the lane narrows to a wide path. Cross over the road at the top of the hill and immediately opposite there is a footpath sign, 'Hat Lane ½ mile, Wiggle 1 mile'. Follow the path over a stile and then another into a field where you keep straight ahead, uphill. Turn back here to enjoy the view across Cawsand Bay. Make for the house visible ahead. There is a gate and stile. Go over this onto Hat Lane. Cross over to Wringford Farm. You will find an interesting collection of donkeys, goats and sheep here. Just past the farmhouse is a footpath sign on your right. Follow this sign along a path which passes between shrubs to a stile. Cross this into a field, turn left and, keeping the hedge on your left, walk towards a wartime pill box. Bear left onto a track. Turn right towards houses and then left, following a clearly defined path until it joins a lane. You are at Wiggle. Turn left and continue on the lane until you reach the coast road with magnificent views. There is a small car park here. Cross over and look for a Coast Path sign just on your right.

Follow the sign for Rame Head, 1¾ miles. The path is mostly wide with springy turf and easily walked. Pass a hut marked 'Plymouth Wiggle YMCA'. You will shortly pass behind some houses and an old fort and will probably be surprised to see a tennis court here just below the Coast Path. Continue up some steps. Keep right at the junction, waymarked. It is just about here that I saw the deer. Go up another flight of steps to a memorial seat. As you climb up the headland you will round a sharp corner to see the chapel atop Rame Head. This 300 foot high impressive headland guards the western entrance to Plymouth Sound. The ruined chapel, dedicated to St Michael, has walls 3 foot thick. The Coast Path actually avoids the ascent but it is well worth the extra steps to see not only the 11th-century monks' chapel but the stunning views and beaches of Whitesand Bay.

The next part of the walk is superb – wildflowers, summertime butterflies and the change of scenery as you alter course and walk towards Plymouth Sound and Cawsand Bay.

In about ½ mile there is a sign for Rame church. You may like to make the short detour of ¼ mile each way to visit this mainly 15th-century church which was first mentioned 1,000 years ago.

Continue on the well-marked path, ignoring a car park sign on your left. You are now walking on Penlee Point. At a metalled track keep right. When you reach a group of three benches leave the path and walk down to a grotto built into the cliff. It was a former lookout post and

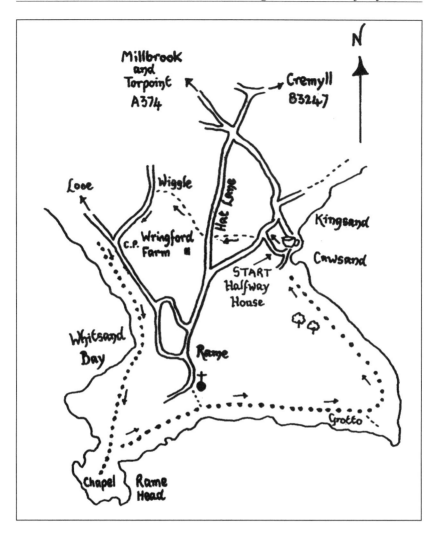

there is a fog signal station here today. Return to the path and continue straight ahead on a wide track. After passing a sign, 'Trinity House Staff only', look for a Coast Path sign on your right. Turn off the track here along a pretty path through the woods which continue until you reach Cawsand. Turn right and retrace your steps through the village back to Kingsand and the pub.

The seafront at Kingsand

 KINGSAND TO CREMYLL (3 MILES)

The Coast Path along this eastern corner of Cornwall leaves Kingsand by following the road to the top of the hill and turning right, along a waymarked path through a field gate. It now runs for 1½ miles with views across Plymouth Sound to Hooe Lake Point where our last walk, from Cremyll, joins it.

CREMYLL
The Edgcumbe Arms

❧❀❧

A walk which includes fine coastal scenery, river paths and woodland tracks, and just one steep climb, in Pigshill Wood. There is much to see en route – Maker church, standing high above Plymouth Sound, its tower used by the Admiralty in the 18th and 19th centuries, St Julian's Well, a 14th-century well house, and the delightful grounds of Mount Edgcumbe House, with sheep grazing in the high pastures while exotic shrubs and trees line the paths below.

The village of Cremyll, the first or last in Cornwall when taking the ferry from or to Plymouth, is dominated by Mount Edgcumbe House and Gardens. The house, built during Tudor times, was heavily damaged during the Second World War. Thanks to the Sixth Earl and Countess it was rebuilt faithfully to the original style. The lovely grounds were landscaped during the 18th century and follow the designs popular at that time. Follies and ornate seats complement the formal gardens, which are surrounded by dense hedges of ilex oak to help combat the effects of sea and wind. Exotic shrubs from all over the world bloom in these protected areas. The gardens and parkland are open throughout the year.

Known as the Passage House until 1730, a name which reflects its position at a ferry point, the Edgcumbe Arms then took the name of the Earls of Mount Edgcumbe. Its history includes accounts of smugglers being summarily tried at a court held here, the judge having been rowed across from Plymouth. Perhaps a rough crossing may have had some effect on the sentence passed!

The pub has been refurbished to a high standard and comfortable furniture adds to the ambience created by sympathetic modernisation. The pleasant garden is a good place to sit and watch the constant movement of water traffic in and out of the port of Plymouth. A blackboard menu announces the daily 'specials', which include a variety of dishes from traditional pub meals to local specialities. Crab or smoked mackerel salads are popular as are the generous helpings of cod and chips. Puddings, served with thick clotted cream, are almost a meal in themselves. St Austell Brewery ales are on offer – try Tinners, Trelawney Pride or a glass of mild. The usual lagers are on draught or bottled and there are good house wines. This last inn on the journey along the Cornwall Coast Path brings it to a satisfactory conclusion. It reflects the traditions upheld by the English village pub, particularly those I have used along this route.

Opening times: 11 am to 11 pm during the summer, 11 am to 3 pm and 6 pm to 11 pm during the winter. Telephone: 01752 822294.

- **HOW TO GET THERE:** From Plymouth (Admirals Hard, Durnford Street) you can travel by pedestrian ferry. There is a free car park adjacent to the ferry. Via Torpoint car ferry follow the A374 to Antony, then the B3247 to Millbrook and Mount Edgcumbe. The pub is just past the car park for the house and gardens. From Liskeard follow the A38 to Trerulefoot roundabout then the A374 and the B3247.
- **PARKING:** Limited parking at the pub but there is a small car park opposite and another one about 100 yards away which serves the house and gardens of Mount Edgcumbe.
- **LENGTH OF WALK:** 3½ miles. Map: OS Landranger 201 Plymouth and Launceston (inn GR 454545).

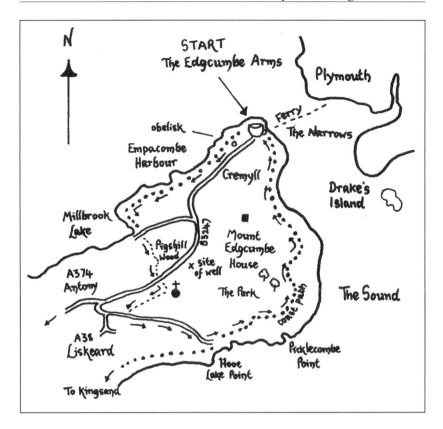

THE WALK

From the pub turn right and take the path between the toilets and the pub car park, signed 'Empacombe ¾ mile'. This path soon becomes a wide track and passes beside an obelisk. There are estuary views from here. On reaching a gate into a field cross by the lower path towards a stile in the right-hand corner. Go over this, when you will enter woodland to reach another stile followed by a gate before arriving at Empacombe Harbour. Note the directions on a gate and follow the path round in front of a row of houses and passing a castellated wall to a stile close to the water's edge. This pretty little backwater encourages one to linger and view the variety of boats moored here and up towards Millbrook Lake.

The route now makes its way through trees then a field towards a stile leading to a lane. Cross over, where immediately opposite you will see a sign pointing across the field which says 'Maker Church ½ mile'. It is tempting to take the wide track here but instead of doing so follow a course towards a clump of trees to the right. Keep to the left of the trees and join a sunken path towards a stile. Go over this into Pigshill Wood. Turn sharp right through the wood, following yellow arrow waymarks. The path winds steeply uphill. On reaching a cross-track, go straight ahead where you will soon see a wooden fence and some steps leading to a road. Cross carefully here and, just opposite, you will see a sign for Maker church. Walk towards the church. A detour can be made here to the site of St Julians Well by walking about 200 yards to your left. You may also like to visit the church on Maker Heights before moving on towards the stile to the right of the church in the hedge about 100 yards along. Waymarked to Kingsand, you may well feel that this will be heading in the wrong direction. However, our route goes this way for the next mile or so. On reaching a lane turn left and continue downhill until you reach a wide bend. You are now at Hooe Lake Point. The Coast Path for Kingsand turns right here but we keep to the lane for another few yards where Coast Path and Mount Edgcumbe Park signs are on your left. Enter the park by this stile and turn right.

 You have now joined the Cornwall Coast Path. The route from here is never boring. Glimpses of the Sound, private paths leading to shoreline properties, secluded summer houses and magnificent trees and shrubs. The route is along a wide carriage drive until you reach an archway above Picklecombe Point. After passing through this arch continue along the track until you see a Coast Path sign directing you downhill through trees towards the shoreline. You can continue along the track if you wish. It will lead you to the house and main drive. Our route, however, follows the Coast Path. At a fork take the lower path, keeping the pond and classical temple on your left. You will pass old battery fortifications and continue between hedges with gardens on your left. On reaching the Orangery, where light meals are served, walk across the gravelled entrance to the main gates and so to the pub.

CORNWALL COAST PATH

This concludes the journey along the Cornwall Coast Path – 268 miles of spectacular coastal scenery where you will have encountered steep cliffs, sheltered valleys, rock formations of immense grandeur and a selection of pubs in which I am sure you have met with a warm welcome, good food and pleasant company.

INFORMATION AND ACCOMMODATION

Cornwall Coast Path

Tourist Information Centres

Camelford: 01840 212954

Bodmin: 01208 872207

Newquay: 01637 871345

St Ives: 01736 796297

Penzance: 01736 62207

Falmouth: 01326 312300

Accommodation

Morwenstow - Cornakey Farm: 01288 331260

Polzeath - The Oyster Catcher (Self Catering): 01208 862371

Perranporth - The Seiners Arms: 01872 573118

Portreath - Su Haili (Guest House): 01209 842110

St Ives - The Croft (Self Catering): 01736 797473

Pendeen - The Radjel Inn: 01736 788446

Treen/Porthcurnoe - Treen Farm: 01736 810253

Perranuthnoe - The Victoria Inn: 01736 710309

Mullion - The Old Inn: 01326 240240

Cadgwith - The Cadgwith Cove Inn: 01326 290513

Portloe - The Ship Inn: 01872 501356

Charlestown - The Rashleigh Arms: 01726 73635

Polruan - The Lugger: 01726 87007

Kingsand - The Halfway House: 01752 822279

Youth Hostels

Elmscott: 01237 441367

Boscastle: 01840 250287

Tintagel: 01840 770334

Perranporth: 01872 573812

Treyarnon Bay: 01840 520322

St Just: 01736 788437

Penzance: 01736 62666

Coverack: 01326 280687

Falmouth: 01326 322435

Boswinger: 01726 843234

Golant, Fowey: 01726 833507